RUSSELL HUSTED

Russell Husted

Hey Mom, What About Dinosaurs?

WINEPRESS **WP** PUBLISHING

© 1999 by Russell Husted. All rights reserved

Printed in the United States of America

Packaged by WinePress Publishing, PO Box 428, Enumclaw, WA 98022. The views expressed or implied in this work do not necessarily reflect those of WinePress Publishing. Ultimate design, content, and editorial accuracy of this work are the responsibilities of the author.

No part of this publication may be reproduced, stored in a retrieval system, or transmitted in any way by any means—electronic, mechanical, photocopy, recording, or otherwise—without the prior permission of the copyright holder, except as provided by USA copyright law.

Unless otherwise noted all scriptures are taken from the King James Version of the Holy Bible.

Verses marked NKJV are taken from the New King James Version, Copyright © 1982 by Thomas Nelson Inc. Used by permission.

Verses marked NIV are taken from the Holy Bible, New International Version, Copyright © 1973, 1978, 1984 by the International Bible Society. Used by permission of Zondervan Publishing House. The "NIV" and "New International Version" trademarks are registered in the United States Patent and Trademark Office by International Bible Society.

Verses marked TLB are taken from The Living Bible, Copyright © 1971 owned by assignment by Illinois Regional Bank N.A. (as trustee). Used by permission of Tyndale House Publishers, Inc., Wheaton, Illinois 60189. All rights reserved.

Verses marked RSV are taken from the Revised Standard Version of the Bible. Copyright 1946, 1952, 1971 by the Division of Christian Education of the National Council of the Churches of Christ in the U.S.A. Used by permission.

ISBN 1-57921-234-4
Library of Congress Catalog Card Number: 99-63731

Dedication Page

. . . for all the prodigal sons and daughters who would come home . . .

Contents

Introduction
You Might Ask, "Why?" vii

Chapter One
In the Beginning 21

Chapter Two
Some Acts of God 51

Chapter Three
Let the Earth Bring Forth . . . Life 73

Chapter Four
What About Dinosaurs? 117

Chapter Five
What About Man? What About Adam? 141

Chapter Six
What About Adam? What About Eve? 167

Tables and Charts
Table 1 155
Chart A 205
Chart B 206

INTRODUCTION

YOU MIGHT ASK, "WHY?"

I was washing the vegetables, getting an early start on dinner. I hoped to finish the job before the children got home from school, but when I heard the front door slam shut, I knew I hadn't succeeded.

"Oh well," I sighed, drying my hands. It was always such a joy to have them home, I really didn't mind at all. I'd rather know they were safe at home and be getting some hugs and kisses while they filled me in on their day.

Jimmy was always the first one to appear, cruising the kitchen like a hungry shark looking for a snack while his more fastidious sister put her things away.

"Hey Mom!" he hollered, well before he arrived in the kitchen.

"Hey Jimmy!" I answered.

"Mom, is the Bible true?" That one stopped me short. I hadn't expected anything like that. The usual was more like "What do we have to eat?"

"Of course," I answered a little pensively. "Of course the Bible is true."

"How do ya know? How ya really know it's really true?"

"Well, it just is. It's the Word of God. Everything God says is true."

"Then what about dinosaurs? We studied dinosaurs in school today. Yuh know, they lived a million, maybe a billion, years ago. Mr. Donnely told me, when I asked him, that the Bible was only a few thousand years old and that dinosaurs were here long before God."

I didn't know what to say. I felt a little overwhelmed. Mr. Donnely and all; how could I argue with him? Jimmy kept right on.

"I went over to Billy's house too. He said I could come right back. Can I? He has this neat program on his computer. It's all about dinosaurs. Billy's dad is home today, and I asked him, too. He said that dinosaurs aren't even in the Bible. He said God musta forgot about them, cuz everybody knows they were there."

By this time Jimmy had arrived at the kitchen table. He started into the crackers and peanut butter I had set out. I watched him devouring his snack while I frantically searched for an answer. I felt a little queasy. I never did understand about dinosaurs, either. I finally just stuttered, feeling quite helpless.

"Uh, well, honey, I . . . I just don't know much about dinosaurs. I'm sure they're in the Bible."

"Billy's dad doesn't think so. In fact, he says there's a lot of things like that, that the Bible ain't right about. And they go to church!"

"Well, honey . . .," I stammered, still at a loss for words. I didn't know the answer, but I did know, in my soul, that he needed one. That somehow, and soon, he needed to get an answer. I whispered a quick, "Oh Lord, help me." But there was only silence. The only thing I could think to do was the oldest stall-for-time trick in the book. And I hated myself for using it.

INTRODUCTION

"Honey," I told him, "I'm sure your dad . . ., well, when he comes home, he'll talk to you. I'm sure dinosaurs are in there . . ., I think. Uh, before you go back over to Billy's, I have some things I want you to do. You'll have to wait until after dinner."

You know you don't have to be as young as Jimmy or still in school to ask the sorts of questions Jimmy asked. You don't even have to be a Christian. In fact, if you were an adult, evolutionist scientist (as I was) you could—rather, you should—still be asking them. Why? Because the Bible's "theory" of Creation is the only other serious competition to the evolution theory (or more precisely, theories) of creation. But when you do ask such questions, the last thing you should have to get for your effort is answers that are less than the best and less than the whole truth. You shouldn't be rewarded with answers that are based on language, concepts, and knowledge that are about four hundred years old!

The problem is, however, that's about all any of us have ever had available. When we've turned to the Bible and read the Creation account, given in Genesis 1 and 2, to see what the Scriptures tell us about Creation, and to study and evaluate what the Bible says God did, none of us have been able to know what that account actually says. None of us have had anywhere near the whole and accurate truth that was first recorded there. Why? Because none of us have had much more to go on than a translation and interpretation—of the Hebrew original—that's about four hundred years old! Four hundred years before modern science. Four hundred years before modern English. And to make matters worse is the fact that the original text, being translated and interpreted, was written in a 3500 year-old, pre-any-science-like-we-have-today, version of Hebrew! Might we see at least a few disadvantages here?

Now, when most of our children go off to school (even to a "church" school), they are going to be taught the very latest, up-to-date stuff in the sciences. That certainly includes evolution. In fact, they are generally going to be taught (quite explicitly taught, and required to agree, if they want to pass their exams) that evolution is a fact. Few scientists, and even fewer teachers, ever think of evolution as "just a theory" anymore. To them (and this will be what they honestly feel obliged to teach their students), evolution is as much a given fact as Creation is to a Christian who believes in God as the Creator. The only thing they think is still theoretical (that is, hypothetical and not a proven fact) about evolution is some minor details like, "Were dinosaurs hot or cold blooded?" and "Did it all start just a billion, or perhaps fifteen billion, years ago?"

They are also taught, again and again, that modern science and the theories of evolution effectively contradict the Bible and Genesis 1 and 2. It's been apparent for decades, now, that such teaching is leading many Christians to doubt the Bible, and to distrust both its truthfulness and usefulness. Many, many Christians now doubt even the possibility, not just the probability, that God is our Creator. That's why it is too important for you to wait until your own children, or even you, are led into untruth or disbelief, and to a place where you don't even want to give the Scriptures and the Creation "story" a fair hearing. You don't want to be found in a situation like Jimmy's mother.

Don't just think of it as her problem! If you were the father coming home in another hour or two, would you be able to do any better? Do you know where the dinosaurs are in the Genesis Creation record, or if they are in there at all? Do you have any idea what God actually tells us about genetics or species? Would you be surprised to learn that what science calls evolution is actually addressed in the Scriptures, and may well have a place in the scheme of Creation? Do you know how well the order of appearance of life

INTRODUCTION

forms given in the Genesis Creation account does match up with the order of the "origins" of life forms that most scientists believe is revealed in the fossil and geological records?

I can answer for you. The truth is, you don't know those things! The truth is—and that's the reason for this book—neither did I. In fact, not one of us, Christian, scientist, atheist, theologian, child, or adult, has ever really known exactly what the Bible says in the original, in the Hebrew Scriptures writ of old. That's because no one has ever seriously and thoroughly gone back to the original Scriptures to see how they read precisely, and how they measure up against what modern science is out there discovering and declaring today!

Every day the modern science "story" is being updated and improved. The latest discoveries in the fossil record, in genetics and biology, and in physics and astronomy—all the latest discoveries and latest theories in a host of sciences—are being extremely well presented and broadcast in the schools, and in the newspapers and magazines, movies, and TV documentaries. They are well known and generally accepted by just about everyone. Who nowadays, for instance, doesn't believe dinosaurs were real some millions of years ago?

Yet while all this is going on, the other "story," the scriptural record of the Genesis Creation account, is still being seen and understood, essentially in the perspective of 1611 A.D., the time of the King James translators. Oh, to be sure, there have been lots of new versions and translations of the Bible in recent years. Everyone, it seems, is bringing out new interpretations of the Greek and Hebrew texts, reworking them into modern language and special contemporary themes, even incorporating the latest historical, archeological, and sociological facts and wisdom. But that has been almost entirely dealing with the New Testament and the historical accounts of the Old Testament. The Creation account, Genesis 1 and 2, has been left all but untouched. No one has re-examined and redone the "science" that was presumed, or ignored, in the King James account of Creation. Think about that. Even if it told us that God created dinosaurs (or genes), not one single person in 1611 would have had any idea of what a dinosaur (or a gene) was. There wasn't even a word for such things invented yet! So how could they have interpreted the Scriptures correctly?

The problem, here, is not the correctness or accuracy of the Scriptures. We haven't gotten that far. We're still dealing with the correctness and accuracy of our interpretation and understanding of the Scriptures! We may well believe the Scriptures are timeless truths, but we have yet to discover what those truths are, because we have not yet translated them correctly. The science and language of 1611 was not up to discovering and expressing their timeless truths about the Creation. Indeed, we might still not be up to the whole job, but we are definitely in a much better position than they were in King James' time!

In King James' time, the needs and purposes for which the Hebrew was being translated into English were very different. The King James Version is a very poetic, literary translation. The 1600's were long before the age of science and Evolution (the capitalization is used to refer to both the scientific theories and, essentially, religious beliefs that go along with the ideas of evolution for so many folks). They not only did not have the language or the knowledge to translate Genesis in such a way as to answer scientific questions; they did not have any need or purpose to do so. We now do have such needs and purposes.

It's a shame, I think, that some scientists have not stepped forward and helped us. But then, that would be asking a lot. Why should anyone want to go out and look for a contradiction to one's own favorite beliefs and theories? What reasonable scientist would like to discover, by dint of his or her own hard work, that a 3,500-year-old book "beat them to the punch" and presents a very sound theory that fits modern data every bit as well as their own?

So they've left the four-hundred-year-old King James rendition alone, happily accepting it as "the correct translation." If it is accepted as accurate, there really is little left to debate. It's been an easy "straw man" target for atheists, proponents of evolutionism, and anyone else who wants to see the Bible retired and out of print. There are, to be truthful, quite a few scientists who do have doubts about evolution and think Creation may be a better explanation of our origins. But lacking a truer translation of the Genesis Creation account, and not wanting to go up against the politics of funding, tenure, and publication, most scientists keep it to themselves.

Well, that's history now, and complaining won't help. We just need to get on with fixing the problem ourselves. We need to revisit the Genesis Creation account with a modern, scientifically informed perspective. This current generation of moms and dads, and the coming generation of young students, are the ones who most need to know the truth.

There are quite a few good books available that reveal problems and fallacies in the science and theories of evolution, but few are written in plain language. There are also quite a few books that defend the biblical account of Creation, as we presently understand it. But in the end, given our present version of the "story," most of them end up little more than "as for me, I will believe . . ." defenses. That's what I call "circling the wagons."

Modern kids want proof and logic, not just a "Well, that's what I believe." Even some bright scholars who call themselves "scientific creationists" have failed to do the job. They try to use scientific methodology and some selected modern data to make what I see as essentially another "circle the wagons" defense. All of them, at their best, are still trying to defend the King James picture of Creation that was painted in 1611.

What you're going to find here is quite different. In this book, we will look behind current Bible translations to the original Hebrew Scriptures. There, I think you'll see that the Bible "said it all" 3,500 years before science did. It will be shown that the Bible gives a precise and accurate outline of the history of Creation and the appearances (origins) of life. You'll also see that Genesis is remarkably in accord with the history and outline of origins that most modern scientists now accept—if we disregard the evolutionist theology and any definite timetable. Not only that, it's getting closer! The latest in science is converging ever more closely with the biblical account. The Bible will also be shown to have set forth some surprising fundamental principles that match our modern understanding of genetics, species, speciation, and so on, which are all things that bear directly on the fundamentals of evolutionary theory.

This work is not a condemnation of the King James or any other Bible versions. As I already noted, the needs and challenges the church faced in the 1600's were very different from those of today, and the messages they needed from the Scriptures were very different. In these times, science and scientists have almost become objects of worship, and Evolutionism has become a veritable religion, and the evolution-as-fact doctrine is one of the greatest challenges facing the Church and Christians. Answers for these kinds of problems are what we will seek from the Scriptures in this book.

One can almost picture the King James Version as a toreador, unaware a second bull has entered the ring! This second bull, Evolutionism, has a pair of very long and sharp horns known as modern science and the information-age. They both cut deeply and quickly, drawing the blood and vitality from our faith and belief. The new bull has been blind-siding the King James Version, and all of us, since about 1860. This book is stepping into the arena to help. To join the fight. To parry and face down the new bull of Evolutionism that has savaged so many of our children.

Neither is this work just another "defense" of Creationism. The Scriptures and the "story" of Creation should need no defense, if they are what they claim to be. I have assumed, in order to keep the translation and interpretation relying on the Hebrew text rather on science or ideas proposed by modern authors and authorities, that the (original) Bible is factual and accurate—a veritable textbook written exactly as the Author intended it. And I assumed that the Bible is not old-fashioned, outdated, or irrelevant because of the works of science. It is only the linguistic and cultural-colored lenses of previous translators that are a bit old-fashioned and outdated.

So this book is intended as a straightforward, disregard-what-the-other-guys-have-said translation of the first and most authoritative textbook that there is on Creation. Its 3,500 years of antiquity are no reason to prejudge it as "surely outdated" or "surely unsupported by the latest evidence." In fact, its 3,500 years of antiquity are a good reason to respect it as the "one to beat," especially when we can show that it predicted the latest evidence long ago.

Prediction, as you know, is the most fundamental axiom of good science! The paradigm (model and theories) of evolution, however, is pretty much practiced in reverse. Most evolutionists constantly use ad hoc and after-the-fact explanation, instead of prediction. They look at the latest fossil finds or biological facts, reflect and think a little, then declare, "Of course, just as we thought!" They will always make the latest finds a perfect "fit" in their evolutionary story, precisely because they already "know" it had to have evolved. Period. The "story" (of evolution) is constantly being rewritten to fit the new fossils and discoveries in the biological sciences to maintain and justify the obvious ending—that whatever exists here and now (or once did), evolved to what it is (or was). "Evolution" (small "e") has simply replaced

"Creation," and "Evolution" replaced "Creator." That's not prediction or good science.

The Genesis Creation account, on the other hand, was written 3,500 years ago. It already presented its paradigm of Creation 3,500 years ago. It can't be changed. Whatever it predicted we would find (say, how the fossil and geological records or evidence about the beginnings (the "Big Bang") of structure of time and the universe, etc.) cannot be adjusted and rewritten as the modern paradigms are. The way that the latest evidence falls into place either confirms or contradicts the "story" in Genesis. Thus, the Creation account stands as genuine prediction and can be treated as straightforward hypothesis. Science, as it accumulates the facts and data and builds better and better theories about origins, can itself either support or contradict the "theory" in Genesis. We can't rewrite it looking backwards. We can only make sure (by some intelligent and honest retrospection) we've translated it fairly! I think you'll be surprised to see how much science is now beginning to support the Genesis account. And that Creationism, therefore, is not a "theory" on the defense in this book.

There is much to be gained by all of us, friend and foe of Genesis alike, in a true and accurate read of the account, not some four-hundred-year-old interpretation of it! Why? Well, obviously, if God exists, and if God is the Creator of this world and the life upon it, and if Genesis is true, then all reasonable men should want to know the truth. But even if one doubts that God exists and authored this account, if one can find in Genesis a useful and compelling "theory" of our origins with a 3500-year priority, scientific integrity requires that honest and accurate empirical testing continue and evolution be continued also as only a theory, deserving continued testing and development rather than edification into the new canon.

INTRODUCTION

It took me in writing this book, almost two years to work out what I believe are the most accurate meanings of about sixty verses! And sometimes it's been a bit nerve-wracking. Many times a new understanding caught me by surprise. This book, in fact, is quite a collection of surprises—I never knew what was coming next. Every one of those "surprises," however, even when they seemed "so right" by what I knew of science, still had to be verified again and again.

For example, there's one new translation in here that drastically changed the import and meaning of a small, but very well-known and very traditional part of the Creation story. The change was so drastic that I initially decided to leave it out, no matter how much more sense it made. The passage involved is inevitably the butt of jokes and source of scorn in science classes. The new interpretation would certainly end that. But it was so different and such a surprise, even to me, that I worried it would offend many Christians and cause them to miss the rest of the benefits of this book.

I wanted to leave it out no matter how much it would help "sell" the Genesis account to the educated, let's-be-reasonable folks. But something wouldn't let me. I went back to it a dozen times, reading the Hebrew Scriptures. I looked outside the Creation account for other clues, other evidence about the Hebrew language I was translating. I went into Genesis 3 and 4 and beyond, even beyond Genesis itself, trying to find other Scriptures that used precisely the same Hebrew wording that could support and verify this other, new translation. Several times I thought I'd found what I needed, but it would always fail the toughest tests, so I'd give it up again. But the next day, I'd be back on the computer with it. This went on for quite a while. My wife, bless her, put up patiently with my many days of frustration.

Then I received a new inspiration. I went back to the verses involved and dug through the linguistics once again. "Eureka!" I was sure I'd found the answer. But even with strong proof in hand, I got fainthearted. The answer was just too different from "established" interpretations. I still didn't want to go that far.

"You must!" said a very quiet and insistent voice in my conscience. So back I went to check it out again. It looked good, but I didn't trust myself, so I called around looking for some reliable authority in the language, some staunch Christian who knew Hebrew as a native tongue. A name came to mind. A pretty well-known fellow I'd seen on national television a few times. But he and I were strangers. I got him on the phone anyway and explained what I thought I had found.

"No way!" he said, after he read me his Bible's translation. I hung up the phone more relieved than disappointed.

"Go back," said that quiet voice in my conscience. So I looked again. "But he's right," I concluded, "it doesn't work."

"Look again," that prodding voice insisted. "Only this time, look at Ezekiel 41." I looked into Ezekiel 41. It was another "Eureka!" I got back on the phone and called up my Jewish authority again. I directed him to the new verses I'd read. I could hear him muttering to himself as he leafed through the pages. I could hear him over the phone. He kept muttering as he compared several translations and checking every nuance of the original Hebrew. It was quiet for quite a while. Finally he answered: "I can't believe this. I've never seen that before. Why did God say that? I never noticed that. But here it is in two places! I don't understand why, but you're right. This is amazing! I'm going to have to study this some more. I'll get back to you."

As he hung up, I knew it had to go into this book. Since then, I've run it by dozens of pretty conservative Christian associates. I have been delighted to learn it doesn't bother them! In fact, most have been gratified at the new interpretation. Very little in this book actually has met with objection. Still, I think each and every interpretation, whether of a single word, phrase, or verse, can be accepted or rejected independently. And probably should be. We need to keep our inquiry and study open and ongoing.

To help you draw your own best conclusions about each and every point made in this book, nothing about the translating will be undocumented. Every Hebrew word that is being re-interpreted is given and almost tediously translated. (This is the heaviest burden I think you will need to carry—putting up with all those Hebrew words being transliterated in italics—and you can easily pass over them if you want, just reading the results!) You can pick and choose all you want. But unless you reject an awful lot of it, I think you will still gain an extraordinarily new understanding of the Genesis Creation account. If you happen to be one of those Christians who has put that part of Scripture on the shelf in deference to a daunting amount of science and seemingly indisputable contradictions, I trust this book offers the understanding you need to re-establish your faith in the truth and authority of the whole Bible.

I conclude this introduction with a passage of Scripture as rendered by one of the newer translations in the marketplace. It answers the question "Why?" for me. It explains why I wrote this book. It's in Ephesians chapter three, beginning with verse 1, and is taken from The Message, by Eugene H. Peterson (Navpress, 1988):

> I, Paul, am in jail for Christ, having taken up the cause of you outsiders, so-called. I take it that you're familiar with the part I was given in God's plan for including everybody. I got the inside story on this from God himself, as I just wrote you in brief.
>
> As you read over what I have written to you, you'll be able to see for yourselves into the mystery of Christ. None of our ancestors understood this. Only in our time has it been made clear by God's Spirit through his holy apostles and prophets of this new order. The mystery is that people who have never heard

of God and those who have heard of him all their lives (what I've been calling outsiders and insiders) stand on the same ground before God. They get the same offer, same help, same promises in Christ Jesus. The message is accessible and welcoming to everyone, across the board.

This is my life work: helping people understand and respond to this Message. It came as a sheer gift to me, a real surprise, God handling all the details. When it came to presenting the Message to people who had no background in God's ways, I was the least qualified of any available Christians. God saw to it that I was equipped, but you can be sure it had nothing to do with my natural abilities.

And so here I am, preaching and writing about things that are way over my head, the inexhaustible riches and generosity of Christ. My task is to bring out in the open and make clear what God, who created all this in the first place, has been doing in secret and behind the scenes all along. Through Christians like yourselves gathered in churches, this extraordinary plan of God's is becoming known and talked about even among the angels!

All this is proceeding along lines planned all along by God and then executed in Christ Jesus. When we trust in him, we're free to say whatever needs to be said, bold to go wherever we need to go.

CHAPTER ONE

IN THE BEGINNING

Genesis 1:1 *In the beginning God created the heaven and the earth.*

"I*n the beginning . . .*" Now that certainly seems straightforward, simple, and rather obvious, wouldn't you say? Many of us might look at it as just a convenient opening phrase, with about as much significance as "On a dark and stormy night" or "Once upon a time." We'd probably have a hard time imagining that *"In the beginning"* by itself could ever be a problem for someone. After all, we aren't even to the "God created" part! But the fact is *"In the beginning"* has been a serious problem for a lot of folks, for a lot of centuries. Let me tell you about it.

From very early on in the history of metaphysics (the sciences and philosophies about the existence, creation, and the nature of things, often part of the theologies of religions), there have been a lot of people (including some of the most famous in our own culture's history) who have thought that time and space—and probably our universe—are infinite. That is, they believed that there was no beginning to existence. The Bible, not accidentally, set that straight. That's much of what Genesis 1:1 is about. It says, flat out, that there was a beginning. It's only after that point is made that verse 1 can get on with the rest of its message. The verse has two more points to make. First, God was there. In fact, the point to be understood is that God was not just there then, but He was there before the beginning. Why? Because—this is the second point—God was, in fact, the Beginner! He was the initial Cause, the Creator, the One to kick-start the whole shebang! He created the heavens (read, universe) and the earth. That, my friends, is certainly a rather "in your face" set of contentions.

So you see, Genesis 1:1 is not a simple statement. It's a collection of unequivocal and powerful assertions, each of which is enough to challenge the beliefs of many different people. That first bit, *"In the beginning,"* is a plain and simple declaration to many of the philosophies of that ancient (Moses') time, and now to many atheists and the followers of most other religions (nearly all the Eastern religions, such as Hindu, etc., preach eternity as well as different gods). It says, "You're wrong and I'm right!" Then the rest of the verse, for all intents and purposes, sums up the first half of the message the Bible intends to deliver: "There is but one God, and I am that I am!"

But let's learn a little more about "the beginning." For you and me, heirs of Western science and the great conflict between evolution and Creation, that first point—*"In the beginning"*—has its own separate role in history, and it has long been used in and of itself as an argument against the Bible. It will help us further on if we understand a little bit more about why that's been so.

What we call science, today, started out pretty much as a Christian endeavor, in the West anyway. Most of the more famous scholars of a couple hundred years ago, whom textbooks credit as the "fathers" of modern science, were Christian scholars who thought they were going to merely explore, detail, and explain the mysteries of God's handiwork in the Creation. They thought they would make it easy for us to know the truth of Paul's dictum in Romans 1:20: *"For since the Creation of the world His invisible attributes are clearly seen, being understood by the things that are made, even His eternal power and Godhead. . . ."* (NKJV). But in time, somewhat hastened by church authorities who distrusted independent thinkers and were often quite hostile to the new scientists, Science (the capitalization referring also to the community and culture that grew up around science and science practitioners) drifted away from its Christian roots and began to assume, or make a deliberate choice of, atheism. In the 1800's it began coming up with the theory of evolution as its own theory of creation. At the same time it was opting for the theology of an infinite universe.

Not surprisingly, these three pillars of metaphysics (atheism, evolution, and infinity) became blended and mutually interdependent. As the twentieth century began, evolution became the preferred theory and belief system (as much a religion as a scientific theory, for many) of most modern scientists. And Evolution had a few theological necessities of its own. First, Evolutionists needed to show that "Mother Nature," rather than the biblical "Father God," created life. It also greatly helped strengthen their faith and their evangelistic agenda (winning converts throughout society, as well as in science) to demonstrate the Bible was full of error and not just thematically wrong. The debate over whether there was a beginning, or not, was just one part of that. Ultimately, that question is not really a decisive issue for the theory of evolution, but for many evolution-believers, it was of more importance than just a simple matter of fact. It was a matter of faith, or counter-faith.

But, as the century and the theory of evolution advanced, it was also becoming apparent that the presumed mechanisms of evolution (chance mutation, chance benefits in a contemporary environment, chancy "natural selection and survival," the drawn-out processes of accumulating millions and millions of minute changes, etc.—things which we'll look at later, and which, I think, are explained in ways they'll be easy to understand) were very slow and needed lots of time. Bishop Ussher's 6000 and some years, which many Christians insisted was all the history there was, were absolutely impossible. Evolution just never seemed to have enough time.

Evolution was little more than a wandering slowpoke. Theory said it had no direction or purpose. There was no path laid out for it to follow; it could retreat as easily and logically as it progressed. To move at all (accomplish any "evolutionary change"), it continually had to overcome its own accomplishments; that is, it had to defeat the built-in safeguards that maintained the species it presumably had created, in order to resume disrupting and modifying the line of descent it had established—to create new species and genera again. Even hundreds of millions of years were becoming obviously insufficient. If the timeline of life's origins had to be pushed back into what looked like infinity, then so did the beginning of the universe. Almost any beginning, whatsoever, was proving a problem. Physics, astronomy, and cosmology were all enlisted to help in the struggle to disprove Genesis' *"In the beginning . . ."* For about a hundred years, they were really doing a good job. They were winning the debate; so much so that many Christian scientists and theologians were bailing out, abandoning Genesis for Evolution.

As you might guess by my language, however, I'm happy to report that that debate is now about over—resolved in the favor of the Scriptures, of course. The victory was provided by science itself. It began in the late 1800's. An ever-increasing number of accepted theories, which supported or tolerated the infinite universe, were failing to accommodate and agree with new experiments and discoveries in fundamental physics and cosmology (the sciences studying the nature and history of the universe). But it wasn't until a brilliant young upstart figured out a revolutionary new theorem, that familiar $E=mc^2$. That was in 1905 when Albert Einstein, pretty much an atheist himself at that time, developed what is known as the special theory of relativity. With that $E=mc^2$, a virtual intellectual logjam was burst, and a host of related theoretical advancements (including Einstein's next theory, general relativity) flooded the landscape, and science leaped forward into a whole new paradigm (models and theories and what it considers established factual truth). And the consensus was: There had to be a beginning. Nothing about our universe (not time, nor space, nor energy, nor matter) was infinite.

The atheists lost that one. So did their good friends, the evolutionists. Today, they mostly quarrel over the age of the universe and of the earth and details of the time scale for when life first began and progressed through its rather obvious history of orderly appearances. And that's really more their problem than ours, as I hope to show as we go.

Can we trust science will again, in due time, yield to the facts and allow the truth to redefine its paradigm? Perhaps. This time-beginning debate offers some hope that science will move forward again. But there is also serious concern it will not. The biggest problem is that there is a real culture of "political correctness" dominating modern science. That culture protects the more cherished paradigms, and atheism (touted as "anti-supernaturalism") and evolution are among the most cherished.

Science is no longer the most open community. Both membership and success in the scientific community is constrained, much like membership and success in so-called "high society," by an individual's political correctness. We see a lot of that going on right now. In fact, the most discouraging news is that we used to hear criticisms and remarks about theoretical shortcoming from many of evolution's most qualified advocates. The last ten or twenty years, they've been very quiet. Almost no anti-evolutionary thinking even gets a hearing, let alone a chance to earn a livelihood. Still, science is also very egotistical and very competitive, and entrance and success can be still occasionally be won by revolution; by toppling the ruling clique and paradigm. That was the Einstein formula. He finally came up with the undeniable correction, and others soon joined his bandwagon. I believe that's where we come in.

To see the revolution come in the Evolution-Creation debate, which has even stronger religious roots and overtones than the usual science debates, I think it is absolutely imperative we keep up the resistance and demand intellectual honesty. I think it is also absolutely necessary that we offer a much better alternative than we've had so far with our 1600's version of Genesis. For today's debates, we need the most honest and factual interpretation of the Genesis Creation account we can muster. It needs to be a translation that anticipates the issues, uses the appropriate language, and details those tiniest of clues of "science" that were purposely built into the original Hebrew text.

Only then can we and scientists reasonably compare creation theories, evaluate the latest of scientific evidences, and finally topple the ever-weakening theories of Evolutionism. That's the task before us. That's what this book is about. And that's why it's in your hands, because you and your children will be the next generation of scientists and "customers" buying the ideas and philosophies and products that science will have to sell.

In the chapters ahead, we're going to look at Genesis as a "scientific picture" of Creation. Now, the Genesis account is not much more than an outline of the history of Creation. It does add, however, a few very significant details, wrapped in the particular choices and precise ordering of the words which the Hebrew writer employed, about the cosmos and about biology and genetics. But that's all we have. So we've got to be careful to make sure we're only comparing apples to apples, and not apples to oranges, or apples to the whole tree. Since we've only got a bare-bones outline of Creation in Genesis, we will only compare it to the bare-bones outline of creation as most scientists think it happened.

That means part of our job will include stripping away the biases, the interpretations and conclusions dictated by evolutionary theory, of the scientific account. And, we'll pay little attention to any dates and timelines that scientists have attached to their history. Genesis itself, you see, has no time scale. It has an order and sequence of events and those well-known six days (which we'll examine at length soon), but it has no dates attached to any event in Creation. And Genesis has only one "theory," which is simply stated: God created. There is very little explanation of how the creating was done or how it proceeded, though the text is not without at least a few clues (which science could legitimately hypothesize and investigate).

So if we look only at the data which science has gathered in such areas as the geological and fossil records and compare only those few details about astronomy, biology, and genetics that are inferred or provided in Genesis, ignoring the interpretations and explanations of evolutionary theorists, we'll be comparing comparables and seeing just how the Creation theory of Genesis lines up with, and predicts, what the scientists should find. I also think that you will see just how that old historic relationship between the world and the Word that science once believed in and worked with, still works.

That's the agenda here. The end results, I think you'll find, add up to a remarkable set of similarities and correspondences that deserve to be evaluated as evidence for the Genesis Creation theory. As I see it, if the Author of Genesis, some 3500 years earlier, successfully set forth an outline of the history of the Creation, and included some further significant details and characteristics of that Creation that modern science is only now coming to recognize (sometimes very reluctantly, such as in the *"In the beginning"* debate), then surely the Author's "theory" should gain some respect, if not full credence.

So let's get back to interpreting our first verse in Genesis.

Genesis 1:1 *"In the beginning God created the heaven and the earth."*

Okay, we've begun to understand what Genesis 1:1 has to say. It tells us that before there was time, before there was height or width or any dimension of space, before there was any physical or material thing, before there were even any natural laws about things (such as gravity, $E=mc^2$, the constant speed of light, et al.), God was there!

You see, before the universe (the earth and the heavens around us) existed, there was no matter or energy, so likewise, there weren't any rules or principles about how things such as matter and energy and even dimensions (including time) would interrelate and interact. Most scientists and philosophers now accept that idea. Conceptually, they understand (I guess) that their mathematics, their theories, and the Scriptures all agree that there was a time when time began, and that before then, there was nothing. As we've said, time and the universe don't go back forever. There was a beginning.

Once begun, or nearly then (the best evidence and theories seem to reveal that it was within the tiniest fraction of a second after the beginning), all the energy and matter that now exists, existed. There was still much to happen (and there is still much happening), but the rules and principles by which everything was going on were also set in place and remain the same now.

That is, galaxies and planets and suns had to form and take their places throughout the reaches of the universe, and they are still doing that, but the natural laws, which govern how they will do so, are unchanging. Now this is not a minor point! These principles, rules, and laws about the properties of things and the ways they interact and interrelate, have no explainable or predictable reason for being what they are. They are totally arbitrary rules that came along with the rest of the Creation, starting from nothing, and being absolute and totally in place—just because. To be sure, they might be thoroughly consistent and rational and well integrated (so far they appear to be), but they are still simply arbitrary. What they are, and their reasons for being what they are, are merely discoverable. Something, or someone else, made them what they are.

We don't make them or affect them; we just try to discern them. Interpret them. Use them.

But concealed within what I just said, lies a basic truth that science depends on. Scientists assume that the Creation is lawful, that reality is not merely quixotic or irrational. They assume that the nature of things and the laws of nature are consistent and constant, and may be discovered and deduced by our accurate observations and reasoning. Such discovering and deducing is what science is about, and is being rather successful at, in most fields.

Those assumptions are the absolute, rock bottom foundations of science. Scientists must work with the assumption of logicality and rationality in the order and rules (natural laws) of the universe. Scientists also have to trust, or assume, that the rules are consistent and fixed, that they will not shift or prove unreliable. If that is not the case, there is no point to science. Science fiction and fantasy fiction tells you what existence would be like if the natural laws and rules were not rational or fixed. Anything could happen, and probably would, tomorrow!

Both of those assumptions, you might notice, are more hope than certain fact. In the old days, when science was just beginning, scientists were confident of such hopes because they were sure of the source—they were sure the source was God. They were equally sure that God was absolutely rational and reasonable, and that He was the source of all order and law within the Creation. They believed Romans 1:20, and they believed the many Scriptures that tell us God and His Word, which created the universe and maintain it, are dependable and never changing. As you know, most scientists do not have that faith any more.

Without that previous faith in God, but still in need of the same confidence in their assumptions, science is presently on some philosophically (metaphysically) shaky ground. Instead of an intelligent and caring God, most scientists have had to build up a new faith in something they call "nature." But nature is, by their own definition, a brute force, unthinking, without purpose, and wholly uncaring. (But this same nature is still given credit for creation, designing evolution, and supplying even our souls and minds!) I think many scientists would welcome the return of God into their metaphysics.

I expect that some of you readers might be in that same place. You have also lost faith in the Scriptures. When someone points to the Creation account as the "other explanation" of life and our environment, you might want to make the objection that "It only 'says' so. There's no 'proof.'" Well, you're going to have to read the rest of this book to see if that's true—if Genesis is only asserting with no proof. We will be treating Genesis pretty much as a textbook. We'll try to read it very carefully to see exactly what it says, in fact, and in implication. And as we do, we'll test it against the facts and data of the "real world," as modern science now thinks they are doing. That's how you develop proof. You accumulate agreements, data that fit and agree with explanations and predictions. And that's all we should do with any science textbook as well.

When a textbook in our classroom teaches the scientific equivalent to Genesis 1:1: "In the beginning, a 'Big Bang' created the heavens and the earth," the authors don't know that for a fact. That's a theory that someone, or several scientists, invented to fit a few facts and data, and to stay consistent with a few other theories they also presently accept. The "Big Bang" theory that is so popular, nowadays, is strictly a matter of belief, period. Like all belief, it's a matter of choice. The facts and data that lead me to God, instead of the "Big Bang," are what the rest of this book will be revealing.

So let's pick up where we were going with our interpretation and analysis of Genesis 1:1. We've made the point that to be the creator, God had to be there first. Before time and space or any other substance or dimension existed. He had to "be" before the beginning of Creation, so He had to be in some other dimension, or set of dimensions. There must be dimensions outside those we ourselves know. Dimensions before time, as we know it; dimensions before space, as we know it; and before mass and energy, as we know them, yet existed. Before the "Big Bang" happened.

That's what is often called the "supernatural," the "outside the natural" of our own experience. But what does that mean? Can you really, seriously picture another dimension, such as something before time, or place before place? Probably not. You never had to before; not in a normal life. But try, for just a minute, right here, as we talk about these (perhaps rather pointless) things that scientists who believe in the "Big Bang" (and the "nothing-something" that was before everything) talk about.

As physicists, mathematicians, and astronomers are probing far back in to the past toward the beginning, searching inside atoms and energy, and peering out toward the edge of the universe, they are now coming to the conclusion that there are other dimensions, more than the four we now experience—especially other dimensions of time! In fact they now know (or believe) there were at least eleven dimensions when things got started. That's seven more than we now normally experience. One of the reasons they believe in those extra dimensions is that without them, especially dimensions of time, their theory about a beginning, the "Big Bang," doesn't hold together. While a number of successful theories (meaning they work, they predict and explain data, and lead to workable new technologies) now rely upon the fact there was a "beginning," the mathematics and principles of a "Big Bang" thing, producing the known universe with the four dimensions we experience, all appear to require more dimensions in their equations. But this all sounds rather "super natural," doesn't it? That is, somewhere or something that is beyond our natural? Well, these modern scientific folks, of course, generally don't like the idea that God is "out there" (as I would suggest) in those other seven dimensions, or that God was there before them, before the universe began. Their solution is to invent or bring in some new non-God concepts and words. So if you read science books, you'll see a word like "singularity," instead of "God" or "In the beginning." And you'll read "Big Bang," instead of "God created." Another translation of Genesis that the modern scientists might want to propose, would read like this:

> Generating 1:1 "In the beginning, a singularity went bang, and everything happened—precisely"

Now, seriously, I don't see the improvement over Genesis 1:1, do you? In just a bit, we're going to look at a couple of other Scriptures from outside of Genesis, which I think will add something our understanding of Genesis 1:1, and our own picture of the "beginning." I think you'll be amazed, then, at how much more sense the Bible, especially the Genesis Creation account, does make. And I don't mean it makes more sense in some general way, but how much more "scientific" sense it makes, how it makes sense of the very data and theories of modern science.

But first, let's continue our look at just Genesis 1:1, in our search for the precise details of what that Scripture says. The King James Version reads:

Genesis 1:1 *In the beginning God created the heaven and the earth.*

Most other, newer translations read just a little differently. For instance, the New King James reads:

Genesis 1:1 *In the beginning God created the heavens and the earth.*

What's the difference? One word. You might think it's a trivial difference, but it isn't. It's another interesting clue that can lead us to know exactly what the original (Hebrew) verse was stating. The difference between the old King James, and the New King James and most other newer translations, is that "heaven" is pluralized. The choice between "heaven" and "heavens" is not simply a matter of style or preference.

The word being translated is, in the Hebrew manuscript, *shamayim,* a very pointedly plural concept. In 1611, when the King James Version was first published, it may be that no one had any good reason to be concerned about the difference. Today, many of us might still consider it pretty unimportant. It may be, but we do now know that the "heavens" are in fact a vast and complex universe, made up of many stars and galaxies and collections of galaxies that stretch beyond our greatest imagination, and the singular "heaven" doesn't quite convey that. "Heaven" doesn't give much of a hint about the fullness and complexity of the Creation. In fact, "heaven" may instead be reasonably interpreted only as that place we go after death. The absolutely accurate interpretation of *shamayim* as "heavens" points us to the greater expanses of the universe and avoids that misdirection. The choice of "heavens" also improves the accuracy of Genesis' descriptions of the "natural universe" we live in and lends support to our assertion that it is a true and accurate creation account of that universe.

Concern over whether it is "heaven" or "heavens" also says something about our attitude and opinion of the Scriptures. If we believe that God was the Author and oversaw the work of transcription with great care and authority (the Jews have always believed that about the Pentateuch), then we should surmise that God was, even in this little detail, purposely being precise and accurate. We should trust that the Hebrew writer obediently transcribed that accuracy and seek to preserve it. Apparently the King James translators overlooked that bit of precision and translated the Hebrew into what they thought was adequate and correct. I believe we have missed that meaningful detail of the message over the years, probably because the King James translators were concerned mostly with "heaven," and not the "heavens."

Another word, in this first verse, *re'shiyth,* is translated as "In the beginning," which is probably quite a good translation. But it's interesting to note that it has another meaning; it is very often translated as "first fruits," Or "choicest thing." So you might read verse 1 as saying, "The first fruits of God's creating were the heavens and the earth." You're doing no great violence to the Hebrew, reading it that way. And maybe it helps somewhat, to establish our idea of what the Scripture is also telling us about our own special place in the cosmos, God's intentions, and how He went about doing it all.

You know, it's interesting that most of us, after we've read the Creation account in Genesis, close the book and go away remembering it as having said "and God created this and God created that." We remember that many things were "created" and attribute each creative act to God. However, throughout the Genesis Creation account, a number of different Hebrew verbs are used to indicate the steps and processes in the creating, and they are not usually the "God created" language of Genesis 1:1. Our English translations actually do translate them with some appropriate variety, but we tend to miss that fact and just remember our "and God created" summaries. We are missing some very interesting details there!

Look again through Genesis 1. There are numerous instances of "let there be," and "let . . . bring forth," followed by the phrases "there was" and "it was so." There are also some "mades" and "formeds." We should not be overlooking these details. We should assume the Author put them in there for good reason! We will learn many times over in this book that paying close attention to the original meanings will tell us a lot of very important details about the nature of the Creation, the Creator, and the creating processes. But we have to give very close attention to the original Hebrew. Our English translations get the message jumbled up and obscured quite often.

In Genesis 1:1, the Hebrew word that is translated "created" is *bara*. This word supplies the most absolute sense of "create" available in the Hebrew dictionary. It conveys the idea of creating from scratch, from nothing, from zero to complete. It tells us that God Himself, in a personal sense, created the heavens and the earth. Not reshaped, not rearranged, not redecorated. He created the universe. *Bara* is in clear contrast to numerous other words available in the Hebrew lexicon that essentially describe such creative acts as "shaping," "fashioning," "letting something manifest," or even "commissioning" or "appointing" something to be made (consider John 1:1–3).

When Genesis 1:1 says God *bara*-created the heavens and earth, it is telling us again, repeating the message of *"In the beginning"*; that He created something absolutely. There was nothing there to start with, nothing that He just reshaped, molded, or engineered. In theology, this *bara*-creation is known as *ex nihilo*.

This *ex nihilo, bara*-creation, of Genesis 1:1 is our equivalent to the "Big Bang," of course. The "Big Bang" is the canonized scientific theory about ultimate origins, about the beginning "in the beginning." Scientists, of course, do not know how anything began. Short of being there (or believing the Scriptures are the direct revelation of God), no one can. But scientists, being the way they are, generally feel compelled to have some sort of theory (guess) about everything, so they've tried very hard to come up with one about this. Considering we are dealing with the very first moment in time, they haven't got much of what you might call evidence, or facts. But they do have a few clues. Among them are some minute, less than microscopic, details in what appear to be the original, or first hardened rock of the earth. There are also some details about the size, shape, and qualities (of what we can see, anyway) of the universe, and about the arrangement, movement, and structure of stars and galaxies, etc. And there are some implications from some of their more well-established theories in physics and mathematics about matter and energy and such.

All these clues have been put together into . . . well, the most widely accepted scientific proposition is approximately this: Everything started at a moment. Sometime. Long ago. At a point someplace in space. Probably in the middle. It was probably violent, because the universe got real big, real quick. That brings to mind the idea of an explosion. A very big one.

You probably see where this all leads. Remember, I said it before in my proposed science equivalent to Genesis 1:1.

Generating 1:1 "In the beginning, a singularity went bang, and everything happened precisely."

That, of course is the "Big Bang" theory. And it presumably replaces God. What in the "bang," or in the whole theory, takes the place of God? The best I can tell is that it has something to do with that "singularity." So what is a "singularity?" Well, technically, it is the smallest thing you can imagine (no, it's actually smaller than you can imagine. It's so small that space even ceases to exist—though it can also begin there), but it is still supposed to include everything of the universe within! And in the theory of Generating 1:1, it sort of explodes. In less than a billion-billionth of a second, the universe just suddenly emerges. Talk about a mustard seed! That one even beats the seed in Jesus' example for being tiny, powerful, and full of potential, doesn't it? (Or is it the same one He was talking about?) Anyway, this "singularity" is more of a mathematical concept than anything real, and it certainly defies anything I can imagine. I expect you can see why I said they invent some pretty strange ideas, attempting to replace the Bible!

Now, after having spoken so poorly about it, it might surprise you to learn I actually have very little objection to the Generating 1 "Big Bang" picture. I have to agree that the moment of the beginning of our universe was certainly a big event. And from our point of view (if not God's), it certainly had to start at some point in time (might as well be $T = 0$), and at some place in space (the center of it all, sounds OK with me). The universe probably did, as the scientists say, get created all at once. Genesis certainly doesn't say otherwise. But you know the Bible is not exactly silent about that event. It speaks of it in a number of Scriptures outside Genesis. But when it does, a somewhat different picture of the nature of the event is painted—not so much contradictory, as simply different. Here are a few verses that represent the Bible's description:

> Isaiah 42:5 *Thus saith God the LORD, he that created the heavens, and stretched them out;* . . .

> Isaiah 45:12 *I have made the earth, and created man upon it: I, even my hands, have stretched out the heavens, and all their host (stars) have I commanded.*
>
> Jeremiah 10:12 *He hath made the earth by his power, he hath established the world by his wisdom, and hath stretched out the heavens by his discretion.*

If the beginning was as literal as the Scriptures here describe it, then rather than "Big Bang," I think it would be more accurate to call it a "Big Whoosh." Nothing was exploded or blown up, but "stretched out by His hands," according to the first textbook on Creation. And quite truthfully, no scientist has any well-grounded, defensible explanation of why it was a "bang," or more importantly, why or how it was initiated. The concept of God causing it, and the scriptural description of it being "stretched out," fits all the same data and gives a much more satisfying picture. It does to my mind, anyway. So I'll go with the "Big Whoosh" label and not argue with the scientists any further on that point.

Though we've just begun, I think you can see how we're going to be working through the rest of the Creation account. What we've done in this chapter with this first verse in Genesis, is what we are going to be doing a lot of in the chapters to come. In just this first verse of Genesis, we've seen there are significantly different ways we can translate and interpret the Hebrew and thereby gain a much more informative understanding of how it truly compares with modern scientific opinions, theories, and established facts. We are certainly not the first to set aside the esteemed King James Version and reinterpret the Scriptures. As we saw in just one example (comparing it with the New King James), there are small, but important differences. Many such differences, which we will examine in the future, will be much greater and much more important.

Are we impugning the integrity of the King James Version or any of the others? I don't think so. We're just reexamining the original language with a different focus. Words can often have numerous meanings. Which ones we take depends on many factors. Among them are our own needs and biases, the context (rest of the statement), and what we think the speaker is intending to say. If we think the Bible is intending to tell us some scientific information, we will look for different clues in its words than if we don't expect any scientific accuracy or purpose at all. And I have heard many Christian scientists, even while defending the Creation account, telling their audience that the Bible is not a scientific text. Well, I think that is their error! You'll have the chance to see if I'm right.

There are other reasons why there are many different translations of the same Scriptures and why some of ours are going to be different. One problem for all translators is the fact that the Hebrew language in which the original Genesis account was transcribed is an ancient and archaic language that essentially "died." It wasn't spoken for a long time. It has now been resurrected again, relying much on working backward from what we now think the Bible said. So the Hebrew is often not informing us, but we are informing the old text as to what certain words must have meant. If a Hebrew word once meant or was intended to signify "dinosaur," but the people resurrecting the Hebrew or rendering the King James Bible, never heard of dinosaurs and had no such word, what do you suppose would be the translation? And what would a modern dictionary (say, Strong's) give as an English definition for that Hebrew word? Would it be something even close? Would it be "monster," or "dragons"?

The Genesis account was transcribed, we think by Moses, some 3500 years ago, in an ancient Hebrew language that was changing even in his times. Every generation, it changed, century after century. Think how difficult it is for us to understand so-called Old

English, such as in the original writings of Shakespeare. The King James Version, less than 400 years old, is similarly hard for us to understand because of its Old English, and thus has been re-translated and "corrected" many times, just to help us out. The King James scholars had a lot more troubles to overcome than just out-of-style language.

The ancient Hebrew, when written, had no vowels, no punctuation, and no clear separation of words. It was writing that was designed to be read aloud by a knowledgeable reader. It probably served more to be a memory prompt than a script. These last two sentences, at best, under those rules would look about like this:

TPRBLSRVDMRTBMMRPRMTTNSCRPTTSLSTSNTNSTBSTNDRTSRLSWDLKBTLKTS

And there are other problems, such as numerous changes in the Hebrew script (the written form of letters), but I don't want to belabor these points too long. However, there is one more point I do need to describe, because it will affect some of the things we do in chapters ahead. That problem stems from the fact that the original Scriptures also had no organization into chapters or verses as they do today. The division of the Bible into chapters was first done about 1550, and the division into verses was done about 1560 A.D. Now those were both extremely ingenious, helpful innovations. The system they set up is pretty similar to how your computer organizes information today, and it allows us all to go to the exact same place in the Scripture, no matter what Bible we use (except some of the paraphrased translations popular today, such as The Message). But, as you might suspect, those divisions into chapter and verse required some good guesswork by somebody and allowed a lot of latitude in that person's editorial decisions. Sometimes those guesses were really bad. I find some of the best payoffs in improving our understanding come when I second-guess, or "armchair quarterback," the "King James team of translators" and their 1550's predecessors and redo the verse or chapter organization.

Let me show you an example. Consider where we are right now. We've just finished Genesis 1:1. At this point, if I'd been delineating the chapters, I think I would have ended Genesis 1 with verse 1. Before verse 2. Of course, such short chapters aren't good literary style, but when you reflect upon the Genesis Creation account, you realize that verse 1 truly is a stand-alone Scripture.

Genesis 1:1 says that God created it all, the entire "shebang." Period. Verse 2 then takes on an entirely new perspective. It zooms us into a completely different point of view. We descend from the inter-galactic point of view into the little blue marble we live on; the lonely little planet hung out in space called Earth. It's a lot like the start of a sci-fi movie, such as Star Wars. First, we are flying through open space with stars and asteroids sweeping by the windshield. We hear (or see written) a brief introduction telling us where in time and space we are. Then we drop down on the planet, or into the opening scene of the story. I hope you get the picture.

That's what I think Genesis 1:1 does, though few of us ever notice. It's a grand opening scene with some vital information that sets the stage and gets us ready to more fully appreciate the story that's about to be told to us. It loses some of the impact that is intended, and some of its message is liable to be missed, when it's treated as just part of the coming chapter.

If the King James people had set up verse 1 as it's own separate chapter, I think it would have told us a lot more. Not just trivial stuff, but important stuff. It certainly would have made it much more clear, and obvious, exactly what God did "In the beginning." It would have set it apart as that very different, special kind of creation *(bara)* that it was, and shown us something else of great significance (which we'll look at soon): that it's actually outside, and prior to, the six "Creation-days." Then, a new chapter, beginning with verse 2, would have helped us recognize just how much of a new place in time and space—and how much more personally focused on mankind and Earth—the rest of the book is. But, again, I should remind you that the King James-era scholars never knew what "time," "heavens," and "the Creation" really entailed. So they quite innocently missed and omitted a few clues that we now need to recover in order to meet our needs of today.

We won't get into verse 2 in this chapter. But we will take a little side trip to start getting you ready for things that are coming. Needless to say, this book is preparing you to deal with evolution. Even though we will ignore it most of the time, you still need to know what it is. Now don't panic at that proposition! A lot of people are "snowed" by the very idea of the "theory of evolution," thinking it must surely be very complex, sophisticated, and above the intellects of most of us. Let me promise you that is not true. The theory is really very simple; it's only some of the scientific defenses trying to shore it up and make it work that are a bit deep and confusing.

Evolution did start out as just a scientific theory. Indeed, most proponents, and certainly most scientists, will still humbly accord it that lower status, if you push them to be precise and honest. But in everyday practice, the principles and rules about theory in science have been drastically bent, if not obliterated, where evolution is concerned. Scientists still test and challenge such theories as gravity and $E=mc^2$ and proudly announce corrections they might discover. But it's different with evolution. Few scientists any longer treat evolution as a mere theory, testing it to see if it holds up, and whether it truly explains and predicts what our senses perceive in the physical world around us (facts and data or evidence). Certainly no one in "mainstream science" (a euphemism for those with good standing in the scientific community) is trying to come up with another theory. They absolutely believe, or must profess to believe, that it is the truth. They consider it a fact.

The only work now going on, for the most part, in evolution research and theorizing, is a sort of in-house debate about, and trying out of, different "how come" explanations for the newest fossil or biological discoveries. Because they are sure they know that these latest finds are part and product of evolution. They're like someone with a picture puzzle who is absolutely confident they have all the right pieces and the right picture. If evolution were still just a theory in their minds, they would be ready to question whether the pieces fit and still question whether they knew the final picture.

No, the truth is, evolution has been elevated to a belief, in fact, a whole system of beliefs, and a theology of personal choice. Most in mainstream science are committed believers. I think this book (and many others) will show that saying "evolution made it" is in no way a superior explanation to "God made it." It's just a matter of what one decides to believe. And what beliefs one chooses is often based upon more than logic or good empirical evidence. It's often more a reflection of the beliefs one grew up with, or those one had to adopt to fit into the society one wants to belong to.

The Scriptures are not mute, irrational, or without at least as much predictive and explanatory power about the finished Creation picture! To truly understand this point and make an intelligent choice between the evolutionist theory of creation and the biblical theory of Creation, you need to understand the theory of evolution. You need to know what the logic and rationale is. Most people don't. Most schoolteachers don't. Most university professors don't. Most of all, those people don't realize, or want to admit, it is just a tenet of "belief" they hold; an "As for me, I will believe . . ." sort of thing. I know. I was quite an evolutionist myself when I taught it in universities and worked on the cutting edge of evolutionary doctrine.

So let's get a very simple lesson in evolutionary theory under our belt. Again, don't panic. Just trust me. It's about the easiest thing you can imagine.

Get yourself a pencil and piece of paper and draw the following things. Or, let me draw them for you.

First, draw a square: ☐

Second, draw a pentagon: ⬠

Third, draw a hexagon: ⬡

Fourth, draw an octagon: ⬛

Finally, draw a circle: ○

There you have it. The lesson is almost over. The next thing you do is study these shapes, noting how they seem to progress, gaining a side at each step, from the crude square to the perfect circle. Now make a theoretical inference (guess) about that. You can argue that from what you see, that you believe the circle "evolved" from a square. That is the logic, the fundamental logic at its simplest, of evolutionary theory! The evolutionist makes that assumption (or declaration): that a set of (he hopes, somewhat similar) objects, or things, are related to each other through some stretch of time, and that becomes, *de facto,* an evolutionary sequence.

You probably think that's just too simple (almost a bit silly, maybe) to be evolutionary theory. Well, there really isn't anything all that profound or complex about the idea of evolution. When we talk about the theory, the Darwinian theory about life's origins and evolution, it's much more the metaphysical and theological baggage that people load into it, or try to get out of it, that makes it so darn complex and causes all the trouble. There's no reason God couldn't use evolutionary processes in the Creation, nor is there anything inherent in the usual way we use the term "evolution" that contradicts God being the step-by-step originator of the history of life. We'll actually be getting into that later, and I think you'll be surprised at some of the things we discover in the Scriptures.

No, the most serious problem with evolution, including Darwinian (and later versions), is that evolutionists simply don't want God involved at all. Not in life. Not in nature. So they do all they can to rule Him out. Try to take the rather common sense idea of evolution and make it a natural law that replaces God. That's all stuff we'll be talking about as we go through the rest of this book. For right now, let's just play around with the basic ideas in evolutionary thinking.

Take, for instance, archeologists. Archeologists are always talking about pottery shapes, and pottery styles, and house designs, and art styles; talking about them evolving through time. We understand the sense of that. We understand that human designers, throughout history and prehistory, might just keep changing their designs (shapes) bit by bit as time goes on. We understand that one can sort the archeological remains into different lines (say villages or cultures) and line them up in order of date. We can accept that they are related and "evolving" sequences, or sets, of artifacts. We might even accept the argument they reflect the "evolution" (that is, the gradual change, and perhaps increasing complexity) of the cultures and the ways people lived.

Another example: Suppose someone says that the modern jet airplane evolved from the flying machines designed by the Wright brothers. Suppose that person goes on to claim, those airplanes ultimately evolved from the horseless carriages and bicycles. Would we be really upset, unwilling to hear the story (theory) out? Probably not. First, I think we understand the idea. Second, we also know from history that the Wright brothers tinkered with cars and bikes and that they literally used parts of them to build their first flying machines. We also know from experience how one idea, pattern, or design leads to another and another, until, at last, we arrive at the design (say, a good airplane, house, or pot) we wanted to create. So we can understand, and seriously discuss, a theory that the airplane evolved from the bicycle, because we understand the logical processes involved and know much of the actual history of the designers.

Suppose we had no such historical accounts. Suppose we were alien archeologists visiting this planet, looking over a lot of rusty, dead remains of machinery, which included airplanes and cars, etc. We might propose a different theory. Assessing the best evidence of design, probable functions, and the environmental needs of land-locked human beings, etc., we might guess that boats led to motorboats (for that first evolutionary step off of land), and then to hydroplanes, and finally to airplanes (a great evolutionary leap forward off the planetary surface). Without certain knowledge of the true history, that wouldn't be such a bad or untenable theory. If we then found a seaplane, it would probably be considered the absolute confirmation of our theory. The perfect "missing link!"

Suppose the alien scientists had no idea that humans existed (they were gone, leaving no fossil remains). They didn't know we had built and used the machines to extend our own abilities.

Instead, they thought the rusty "fossils" were remains of living things themselves. What sort of a history, or theory, do you think that would have led to? Having no idea that there was a creative intelligence that actually designed and created these things, the aliens would have had to figure out some convoluted theory, or bunch of theories, to explain how the machines first got created and evolved into that greatest of species, *Aeroplanus rex!* If they had the stubborn mindset that all things evolved and were inevitable products of natural forces (what else could it be, something supernatural?), they'd never even get close to the truth.

As you can see, while the basic concept and principles of evolution are simple and common sense, applications of it can get difficult and messy. The metaphysical and theological baggage and goals one brings along with it can distort it and lead to very erroneous conclusions.

Of course, most of us, most of the time, when we think of evolution, think of evolution with the big "E." We think of biological evolution, origins and creation, and all the metaphysical, theological, and sociological trappings of Evolutionism. We think of the religious and political agendas of those more interested in anti-Creationism and Christianity than science and truth. As Christianity does already have a history of Creation in Genesis, we are always being confronted with the "story," or "history," that Evolutionism is writing as an alternative to Genesis. And we often confuse that with the theory of evolution—a much smaller package.

Biological evolution is no different in its principle and logic than the examples we've just played around with. It still starts with looking at shapes, and then theorizes a history of relationships.

Charles Darwin, who gets the credit for really pulling together the principles and organizing them into a full-fledged paradigm, started with observations of birds and beaks. Studying a collection of similar birds (one set of "shapes," finches), he compared various "shapes" of beaks, their correlation with feeding choices, and behavior (let a "shape" also stand for a behavior, or an ecological relationship, etc., to keep our model and language simple and consistent). He inferred into the collective patterns of similarities and differences a genealogical history. He conjectured a history that ascribed a common ancestor somewhere in the past, then some historical events that included less-than-absolute-carbon-copy offspring (variation in a species) and changing environments or opportunities in environments. Then, finally he invented a story about a new species self-producing itself and living in those different environmental opportunities ("niches"). He conjectured similar histories for lizards and Galapagos turtles and believed he could do the same for all of life on the planet. In doing this, however, he was attempting something beyond mere natural history; he was also attempting to give support to a non-God metaphysics.

Darwinism (and all its heirs today) is more than the basic theory of evolution. Darwinism goes beyond observing and deducing mere histories—which one could yet argue or assume a Designer and Creator wrote—and seeks to establish a theory (or theology) that nature and life itself is the power behind the pencil being moved and the story line being perfected (or selected). Upholding that greater agenda is why and how so many other sciences get brought into the act, and the whole picture gets so complex and contentious.

The basic principles for each still remain the same. Evolutionists compare the shapes of chimps, apes, and men, for instance, and build upon that foundation their evolutionary theorem. Paleontologists compare the shapes of fossils—teeth, bones, claws, shells, whatever remains they find—and borrow from geology and biology to construct their billion-year evolutionary models and write fanciful stories putting flesh on their stony remains. When the biologist looks at animals, or parts of them, such as hearts, gizzards, muscles, and lower-level structures, shapes are again called upon to establish connection between "related" species and their presumed ancestries. The cell biologist, looking into the microcosm of the single cell, sees the shapes of cells and their various parts and processes, and from them also infers evolutionary relationships. And the biochemists and molecular biologists "see" the shapes of molecules, enzymes, proteins, genes, and such, and construct their own evolutionary paradigms.

The problem in this scenario is not so much the research or science going on, but the fact almost everyone in every science is locked into the same literary genre. It a bit like going to a bookstore and discovering only murder mysteries are being written (or published) nowadays. Everything, to successful authors, will look like crimes, victims, and detectives, because everything must fit into a mystery story. Where would a Mother Theresa-type of character or story fit? She'd have to be murdered, I guess. Or become a master criminal. Well, the same selective seeing, interpreting, and story writing gets imposed in most of science right now. Everything has to look like a piece of an evolutionary story or puzzle and fit in to telling and fortifying the Evolutionist version of Genesis.

Now, for those who read this book with a hostile or critical eye, I readily admit to doing a little injustice to modern science and hardly painting a full and complete picture of all the evolutionary paradigms here. But it should be obvious that I can't; that would both require more than one book and not serve the audience this book is serving. But the broad-brush painting and outline characterization of the science and theory is not misleading. It's a framework we can work with, without being buried in detail and science, as we begin to unveil and interpret the hitherto untold story (history) in the Genesis Creation paradigm.

Our interest, in this book, is really the Genesis story. We want to get it analyzed and told as well as it can be, and understand the parallels, the compatibilities, and the contradictions with the

Evolution story. We're not here to refute evolution, or Evolution, but to re-introduce the theory of genesis in Genesis as truthfully as it was written in the beginning. Thus, our essential need is only to understand the core argument, the logical skeleton, of the evolution idea. It starts with comparing shapes. It theorizes by composing a history. Add natural selection and you have Darwinism. Add genetics and you have neo-Darwinism. Add some more sciences and you have the modern evolutionary paradigm. Add some metaphysics and theology and you have Evolutionism. We may need look at a few more of these add-ons as we go, but we'll do that when and if appropriate.

CHAPTER TWO

SOME ACTS OF GOD

First we read:

Genesis 1:1 *In the beginning God created the heaven and the earth.*

And then:

Genesis 1:2 *And the earth was without form and void; and darkness was upon the face of the deep, And the Spirit of God moved upon the face of the waters.* (NKJ)

Why, do you suppose, we started the chapter like this, inserting that "And then" so obviously between verses 1 and 2, keeping them apart with an "And then"? Well, it's to emphasize again that there's a chapter's worth of differences between Genesis 1:1 and 1:2. As we noted in Chapter One, there's a very obvious change in the narration's point of view, and so we need to be sure to shift our own perspective. Genesis 1:1 speaks from a point of view in outer space. It's not just about our small planet but the whole universe. The subject of the verse is the Creation of the entire universe—the "Big Whoosh." It's a galactic view. It's about something that happened even before the Creation of our own world. If we believe what the scientists think today, Genesis 1:1 occurred some five to ten billion years before the time of Genesis 1:2. And Genesis 1:1 is the last time we'll be looking at so broad a picture and at a time so long ago, from the vantage point of "out there." In Genesis 1:2, we're down on Earth and not nearly so long ago.

From that point on, everything in the Scriptures is about things on Earth, or about things as seen from Earth. We will "see" the earth being shaped and developed but always from very near ground level. We only hover above the water, and we look up at the heavens. We see the sun begin to shine, the moon take its place over our heads, and the stars and constellations "turn on" in our own skies. We watch, with our feet firmly planted on terra firma, the plants and animals—our plants and animals—take their appointed places in our ecological system as it is being designed. We never, ever depart from this earth again.

Certainly, we might wonder about what else took place, if anything, between Genesis 1:1 and 1:2. We're never told. Not in Genesis, anyway. Since neither verse provides any kind of a date or reference to time, we haven't even any idea of how much time has passed between the two verses. If we want to make any guesses, we have to go outside the Bible. This is one place science might be able to help, filling in some absent information and helping interpret the gaps.

Scientists love to speculate about dates and timelines. Time is always a very important dimension in everything they study, and often that's the only thing their theories are about. As for that gap in Genesis, they offer us possible timetables for everything that may have taken place, beginning with the "Big Whoosh" (which they think took place some 15 to 18 billion years ago). We can find histories and timelines for the births, lives, and deaths of the stars and galaxies, whose histories are seen as their normal "evolutionary cycles." And since those cycles appear to end in novae and black holes, and we can see such things spread out throughout all the universe and time, scientists believe we are actually seeing a lot of history, such as occurred in the Genesis gap, through our telescopes. Whether or not the details of the scientists' timetables are right, I think the basic picture they have painted of the nature and grand scale of the processes involved in the forming of the structure of the universe, and the approximate scale of time involved, is valid. If that is so, then I think we can be sure, at the very least, that a lot of creation proceeded and completed over some incredible stretches of time between Genesis 1:1 and 1:2.

Astronomy, and its research into cosmology, can be a pretty exciting spectator sport for most of us. Few things inspire as much awe, or so stretch our imagination, as the reports and images coming back from space from NASA probes and Mars-Landers, and the Hubble and land-based telescopes. Apparently, we all have a deeply seated curiosity about the heavens and really want to know about that part of the Creation—almost as much as the creation of our earth. We all want to know, but curiously, it's the part that's missing from the Genesis account. One will find more about them in Job and the Psalms than in Genesis, and even in them there is still precious little information. I find that a little puzzling and often wonder why God would leave such a void with nothing to help our inevitable curiosity and search for answers.

Well, the truth is that if we look closely and try to make sense of some of the events that are given in the Creation account, we will find that Genesis isn't as silent as we might think. Tucked away in a more thorough analysis of the Hebrew language, and with the aid of our (scientific) observations of the world and universe around us, it gives us a number of clues and directions to look, and even some answers. The Genesis account simply isn't complete. It requires us to go outside, into nature, and to seek additional clues and information from such resources as astronomy and physics. The remark in Romans 1:20 is almost a command, if we really want to understand the Scriptures and the Creator. We will find Genesis telling of things that happened in our skies, for instance, that make the most sense if we realize they were events which were already set in motion, or perhaps coming to conclusion, in that time gap between 1:1 and 1:2. We're going to find this happening, especially in verses 1:2 through about 1:9 and in 1:14 through 1:18.

So we can benefit immensely if we look at some of what modern scientists have learned, and give serious consideration to what they believe they are discovering now, about events and processes that may well have taken place in the time gap of 1:1 to 1:2. They rarely contradict the Bible, but in fact, are becoming quite a source of affirmation of Scripture and evidences for a Creator. Science, more and more, appears to be filling in missing information and helping paint a rather remarkable picture of what the Creator did, even to the point of possibly explaining how He brought it to be. That's especially true in physics and astronomy. For instance, almost daily, new discoveries reveal how the "fortuitous design" of the heavens is beyond any imaginable probability and is a perfect and precise design that allows life and mankind. I recommend you read one or two of the new books on that subject, such as those by Hugh Ross. They are exciting and uplifting!

I mention these things now because I want to make sure none of you are put off by our use of science to translate and understand the Scriptures. God tells us to both study the world about us and see therein evidences of Him and to test the truth of His words—which do include the Creation account. Until the last century or two, all science was about that charge, and today many in science still see that as their proper enterprise. If we wish to use the account in Genesis to explain the world and our proper place in it, then we need to take our best observations and theories back to the Scripture to hone our understanding and confidence of both. Iron sharpens iron; wisdom develops wisdom.

The great debate in our society today is still between Christianity and anti-Christianity, and much of the contest for believers and followers is being fought out in the debate over their respective theories of creation. Evolutionism supplies one theory, neo-Darwinist evolution; Genesis supplies the other, Creationism. Evolutionists have many good textbooks to sell their thesis, and they revise them daily as science supplies new data and understanding. Christians have but one textbook—written 3500 years ago. And unfortunately, we have neglected to even translate it well, let alone incorporate centuries of accumulating information and discovery that might enhance our understanding. We need to catch up.

Do you question calling Creationism a theory? I don't think you should. Let me give a few reasons.

First, it helps level the playing field. For most foes, and many advocates and friends of the book of Genesis, the Creation account has been successfully diminished to the standing of a creation story, or a mere myth. It fails their tests for credibility. That is in part because we have had only the unscientific interpretation available and have little opportunity of showing how it does predict and explain the nature of our world and honest scientific data as well, or better than, evolution. We have to face well-established knowledge from medicine, biology, anatomy, etc., not to mention such things as dinosaur fossils. As we reveal the true Genesis of the Hebrew original, we will do much better at that and merit at least the recognition we have a reasonable "other theory."

Second, it calls out to scientists to test it themselves, instead of ignoring it. It calls upon many of us to do the same. Let it be evaluated against the "real world," that natural world it truly claims to account for.

Third, it calls us to not even settle for this translation given here, but to keep on trying to do better, refining our knowledge and understanding of the original account.

Fourth, it sets the Creation account up, once again, as a guide to research and hypotheses. A lot of Christian scientists still need to know the truth of the Genesis language every bit as much as non-Christian scientists.

Fifth, if we treat it as a theory, then many of the details that it set forth some 3500 years ago can be evaluated as predictions.

Finally, recognized as a theory, the Genesis Creation account regains its civil rights and can again be spoken in public places. It can even be taught in the public schools.

Well, let's get back to our work, now, beginning with verse 2.

> Genesis 1:2 *And the earth was without form, and void, and darkness was upon the face of the deep. And the Spirit of God moved upon the face of the waters.*

When I first started this project, I thought this was an easy one. I followed the usual route of most commentators and readily accepted the usual English translation: *"And the earth was without form and void. . . ."* It looked like a perfect fit with the scientific picture and an easy score for Genesis. You know what I mean. It fit perfectly with that picture we all have of a young planet being born; beginning as a hot, formless (and void) ball of gas, whirling in space, gradually cooling and condensing, eventually turning into a ball of liquids and rocks. I was happy to see that there was Genesis, describing our little Earth starting out just as

SOME ACTS OF GOD

science would have it. So, I said "Great!" and got ready to move on to the next bit of Scripture.

Well, I soon realized there was trouble in "Mudville." The trouble is that this convenient and traditional interpretation doesn't hold up on a couple of counts. First, if we accept the language "without form," we know we must be talking about very early times. The earth would be very young, almost before it was even a ball of gas, when it was without form, or just beginning to gather into a "form," beginning to liquefy and become solid. That would mean the gap between verse 1 and 2 is considerably shorter, and we are hardly ready to be transported to the surface (it doesn't exist yet) for the rest of our narration. But the rest of the verse, talking about the deep and waters, definitely does have us there on the surface. Furthermore, talking about water clearly tells us we do have a fairly mature planet already. A planet, to hold liquid water, must be not only solid, but substantially cooled. So which is it? Have we a young formless ball of gases, or a solid and watery sphere? I think we need to consult the original, see what clues we can find in the Hebrew.

Genesis 1:2 actually reads (in basic words, not including syntax and grammar, etc.): *"Erets hayah tohuw bohuw."* Got that? Let me translate. "The planet Earth had become a desolate wasteland of a place, an indistinguishable ruin." Apparently, we would not have liked it much, but it was already here, already firm real estate, and ready for a far-seeing developer. Now some theologians argue that the "ruin" there, might imply the earth was once a better, or a more "distinguishable," place, and it had degraded. We really don't need to know whether that's true or not, though if that were true, it would mean there was another untold creation history before Genesis 1:2. Then Genesis would be telling about a second creation history. Whatever the case, for the purposes of our study, this verse 2, still does tell us that the earth was already solid and ready for development—if not redevelopment. And it tells us that quite a long time had passed between 1:1 and 1:2. Genesis 1:2 continues:

> ". . . darkness was upon the face of the deep. And the Spirit of God moved upon the face of the waters."

The earth was not only condensed and "solid," it was also covered with water. No land is mentioned; the entire sphere is covered with water. The word the King James Version translated "the deep" *(tehowm),* may refer to something like a "primeval sea." We often think a "deep" is an ocean. But it may very well not even refer to water at all. The word translated "waters" at the end of the verse, however, is definitely a Hebrew word about water. In fact, there is a bit more information than just "waters" in the original word, *mayim. Mayim* means "shallows," "waste waters," "swampy waters." So we should picture here no deep blue sea, no chill ocean, but a planet awash in shallow waters—a huge dirty pond.

This turns out to be an even more remarkable picture than the traditional, commonly held idea of "deep seas" covering the earth. This is an even more excellent fit with what science presently imagines early (cooled, and getting-close-to-life) Earth was like.

Scientists believe that as the earth matured, it became abundantly wet with water. Whether the water came from its own constituent matter, or rained down in some very fortunate ice-asteroid shower, Earth was nevertheless very blessed with water. Most other planets, it appears, are abundantly dry. Liquid water appears, as far as our telescopes and initial interplanetary explorations show, to be very scarce in the universe. But Earth has lots. That's both very interesting and fortunate. You see, water, in essentially every origin-of-life scenario scientists can imagine, is the most vital element. Water is absolutely required for life, both as we know it, and

Some Acts of God

in any other form we can contrive. Indeed, all the various searches for "life" of any form on other planets, that you hear about, are usually little more than searches for liquid water!

Let's resume our study of Genesis 1:2. The verse continues:

> "... and darkness was upon the face of the deep ... upon the face of the waters."

What about the "darkness" there? Might that be telling us anything significant? I think we can count on it! For one thing, it's probably telling us that the sun wasn't "lit" yet! That again says something about time and the gap between verses 1 and 2, as well. Suns, you know, have to "grow up," too, to become suns. At least that's what physicists and astronomers, peering back into time, believe.

What they see going on throughout the universe (which is equivalent to seeing back in time) seems to show that a sun-to-be starts out much the same as a planet, a gassy accumulation, only much bigger. At least, a sun-to-be starts with much more mass (matter and energy) than a planet-to-be. As they begin going through the same "condensing" process, their much greater mass leads to a very different conclusion. Much greater mass means there is much greater gravity, and they become too pressurized (squeezed into too small a space) to cool down, and they heat up, instead. As the processes of condensing goes on, they simply reach a point of ignition, or nuclear fusion, and essentially "light up." They act like nuclear reactors, or bombs, after reaching critical mass. They are, however, beautifully designed bombs that are exploding at the same rate gravity is pulling them back together. They end up perfectly balanced between explosion (blowing up outward), collapsing inward, and they stay around as long lasting, beneficial stars!

In the time of Genesis 1:2, it would seem our sun was still just a sun "wannabe." But the earth itself was already well-formed (not "formless"), even cooled and covered with water. "... *And the Spirit of God was hovering over the waters*" (NIV).

No land is mentioned. Of course, if you've read ahead, you know why.

Before we move on to verse 3, I want to take a moment to explain something I said before. I remarked about physicists and astronomers peering back in time. I said, essentially, that what we see looking outward in space is equivalent to seeing backward in time. It's important you understand that equation.

To astronomers, time is not that much different from distance. That's because as they look through their telescopes, whether light-wave, radio-wave, or x-ray-wave instruments, what they "see" is light, radio signals, or x-rays coming from the things they are looking at—all of which are very long distances away. One of the laws, or rules, of the universe amounts to a speed limit on all rays, whatever type. Light and other rays of energy can only come towards us at the speed of light, which I'm sure you've heard of. Now, when you talk about the distances involved between us and almost everything else in the universe, you're talking big. Even things in our own solar system, our nearest neighbors, are so far away that it takes light—limited to traveling about 180,000 miles per second—a long time to get here. It takes about eight minutes from the sun, hours from some planets, and it takes years—light-years—to get here from other stars. It takes millions and billions of years to get here from the more distant galaxies. It takes from the beginning of time to get here from the very edge of the universe! We might see an image of God's hands if we saw the actual edge of the universe!

If it takes an hour for the light to get here from Mars, then anything we "see" on Mars happened an hour ago. We are actually "seeing" history, as far as Mars is concerned. But it's not history to us until it actually gets here, until it can reach us and, consequently, affect us. Then it enters our present and affects our developing history.

Let me tell it another way. The things astronomers see are rather like yesterday's newspaper, since light and other radiation travels very steadily but under a speed limit. This speed limit on light works like the speed limitations of horses used in the pony express of years gone by. In those days, the latest edition of a Boston newspaper, in the hands of a Dallas reader, was "news" to him, but history in fact. That is, the news being read in Dallas was already history in Boston. In Dallas it might still act as present-day "news." It might still be the basis for present (real-time) events in Dallas (maybe offering money for shares of a company), but it was history (the company had folded a day ago) in Boston by the time it got to Dallas. Time is thus "relative," as Einstein was discovering in the theory of relativity. The result of that fact is that everything we see through the Hubble telescope is history. It's showing us what galaxies and planets looked like long ago. The further away they are, the older the news we get. Hubble pictures of stars, galaxies, and the creative, or coming-into-existence, events it "sees" are probably baby pictures!

Now God knew all of this. He knew how events in the stars would not be seen on Earth for quite a while. I think that explains some rather interesting details in the Creation account that critics misunderstand and try to use to discredit the account. It explains some items much better when we're aware of that gap between verses 1 and 2, and understand that we're already quite a ways into the earth's history by Genesis 1:2.

The next verse in the account deals with the darkness.

Genesis 1:3 *And God said, Let there be light: and there was light.*

Now God lighted the sun. We can just as well believe He caused it by simply using (or allowing) natural processes (which He designed and we call "laws of physics") to do the job; to let that ball of stellar gasses condense until the sun ignited into its light-giving, nuclear-reaction "fire."

Verse 4 tells us something else that makes another excellent match with "scientific sense."

> Genesis 1:4 *And God saw the light, that it was good and God divided the light from the darkness.*

First, I think it is important that we stress here that as a scientifically accurate account, these verses should be seen less as literature and more as precise information. I do not believe we should ever assume something is said in this Creation account merely for style's sake but that everything is precisely intended to supply accurate information and additional clues to assist our understanding. I think God gave us this record to assist our own search for truth (science) and to attest that He is the Author and Creator.

That being said, I don't think we should read this verse as a rather blandly poetic statement that God kinda liked the light and decided to make darkness, or night, too. This is not mere poetic myth writing.

With an eye toward scientific information, I think *"divided the light from the darkness"* suggests that the light was mixed up with darkness like muddy water and needed "separating." "Separating" is the most precise meaning of the Hebrew word *bawdal*, being translated "divided" here.

Now consider this: Before most of the "matter," which scientists believe was scattered (by the "bang") throughout space as gas, dust, asteroids, planets-to-be, and such stuff (they often call it inter-stellar debris)—before this matter condensed and collected together into some orderliness (suns, planets, asteroid belts, meteorites, even "settling" like dust onto planets, or whatever)—light coming toward earth through space would have been muddied up ("scattered" is the technical term) and not much separated from darkness! Whatever light there might be, from stars and hot gasses and still-forming astral bodies like the sun, that light would have been scattered, diffused, and reflected about everywhere. It would be like flashlight beams lost in thick fog, smoke, or muddy water. Or like sunlight in a muddy lake, it casts few shadows and barely reaches the bottom.

It's quite possible that verse 4, with the use of "separated," is clueing us in to some facts of how and when God separated the light from the darkness. It's possible that the scientific picture of the natural history of space is quite correct, and it took place just as scientists think, through time, in that verse. There's no reason not to believe that God used, or simply allowed, the natural laws of physics, like gravity and electromagnetic attraction, to get the job done. He knew full well that His laws, and the properties in the matter He created, would, through time, predictably gather up and gather together all that debris like a cosmic dust collector and cleaner of space. He set the entities (gaseous balls of mass and energy) in place, set them on the path to becoming earth and sun, and set up the processes that "separated light from darkness." And told us about it in His historical account.

Night and Day, which God named in verse 5, could only be meaningful on a fully condensed, solid, and rotating Earth in the now-clear rays from the now-burning sun through a now-cleaned-up outer space.

Remember, in Chapter One, we looked at the "create" verb that was used in God's creation of the universe. I told you, then, that we would want to continue to pay attention to the various "creating" verbs. Let's look briefly back through the verbs of Creation-day one.

In verse 2 there are two verbs shown in the English. They are not active creating verbs, but are referring to something already created. We read in our King James Version that "... *the earth was, and darkness was* . . ." The second "was" is a fictional addition, inserted by the King James committee, hoping to make the text more readable. Forget that one. Verse 2 should more accurately be read: "... *the earth was without form, and void; darkness upon* . . ." The basic Hebrew word used in the original, and translated "was," is *hayah*. It is a form of the verb "to be," essentially. It can be translated as "was," but it more appropriately translates as "became" or "manifested." *Hayah* has a more "future looking," or "happening," sense to it. It conveys a process, a through-time idea of "happened," or "was at that point," in the process. Choosing that particular verb, the Scripture tells us that the earth was indeed fully in existence at that point in time or well on its way. It was no mere ball of gas.

Hayah is also used in verse 3, but in a different form, when *"God said, 'Let there be light.'"* It doesn't say "God made light," as you might guess, nor does it simply say that "at that point there was light." Here, it is the more passive, "Let light appear," or "Let the light now be manifest." That fits well with the ideas we just talked about: that the sun might just now be lighting up and the debris in space just now clearing up enough that the light can clearly shine upon the earth. Then, yet another form of the same verb finishes out verse 3, "... *and there was light."* We are assured, just as planned, light did, indeed, manifest; it did indeed show up!

Genesis 1:3 could almost be made two verses. The first, 3a, would read, "God said, 'Let the light now appear' (on the earth)." The second, 3b, would read, "And light appeared." The advantage to two verses would be that we could avoid the idea that "God threw the light switch, and 'blink!'" Instead, we could allow that the light came on in a process over a period of time. As the sun shrank into fusion mass, and the murky space debris gathered and cleared out, light began falling ever more brightly upon the earth. That would fit the verb *hayah* and indicate a very reasonable scientific picture of how it came to be in natural laws and processes. It does not omit or replace God but allows that God was the Engineer, the Creator, who utilized the very system and laws He set up and continues to sustain and use today. Our existence, I believe, even as it follows those "natural laws" which science has discovered, is an ongoing miracle—and a continuing testimony to a Creator!

In verse 5, the same form of *hayah* again proclaims "there came to be." The second half of the verse is translated: *". . . And the evening and the morning were the first day."* More accurately, it could be translated: "There came to be the evening, there came to be the morning (or "morrow"), the first day," for *hayah* is used twice.

The common way of interpreting this verse is that it frames a literal day, and it leads many people to think the Creation-day is a common twenty-four-hour day. The phrasing is curious, however, as evening is first specified, and the morning follows. That looks more like the break between days than the outline of a day, especially if we regard the daylight hours as a day. (Which is, as it were, what the Jews commonly meant by that word, if they used it for "day.") To earthbound observers like you and me, evening to morning wraps the time of rest between our labors. Verse 5 may signify such a break, a rest between Creation-days, as between the sets, or phases, of Creation. If that were the case, then verses 2 through 4 are a record of the several things that the Creator commanded be initiated or caused to take place. They need not have been all finished, but only begun—time was still necessary for their completion. Verse 5 then signals the end and brackets what could be a very long time following Creation-day one, between and before, the second Creation-day.

In our life, in our world, an architect might show up only on Mondays to outline the week's work for his construction crews. "Creation-days" could have been God's Mondays, and the natural forces of His universe, or some hosts of heaven, or even Jesus (*"All things were made by Him..."* John 1:3) were left to finish the works. It's something to think about. And before we are done, we'll try a couple of other ideas out, as well.

What we read of next, in the sixth and seventh verses, once again fits in quite nicely with what the scientists think happened somewhere in that approximate time of the earth's formation. God makes the sky as part of the atmosphere, with water above and water below, but not much water in between.

> Genesis 1:6 *And God said, Let there be a firmament in the midst of the waters, and let it divide the waters from the waters.*
> Genesis 1:7 *And God made the firmament, and divided the waters which were under the firmament from the waters which were above the firmament: and it was so.*

Now, again, in verse 6, the Hebrew verbs translated as "Let there be" and "let it" are forms of *hayah,* the existential verb that conveys the idea of "let it be," "let it become"—almost "let it happen," as by the force of His natural laws. But in verse 7, we read that "God made the firmament." "Made," here, comes from *asah,* a new creation-verb. This *asah* is much less absolute, less direct or personal, and less "from-scratch" than the *bara* of Genesis 1:1. But it is still far more "creative" and "hands-on" than the more passive "let it be's," etc., of *hayah. Asah* says "make," but it is in the sense of "fashion," "design," or "accomplish." *Asah* also carries in its range of meanings, the idea of "appoint" or "commission," as well as "bring about" or "effect"(note: not "affect," but "effect")!

So now we have a total of three verbs being used in denoting acts of "creation." Each one is different. *Hayah* is almost a hands-off, just letting it come to pass, mode of creation. *Asah* involves either the idea of personally designing something or commissioning something (compared to either doing a portrait, or commissioning one). *Bara* is the more absolute, *ex nihilo* and hands-on verb, which was used to tell of God's initial creating of the universe.

Verse 7, then, has brought us something new. Though the English doesn't exactly reveal it, verse 7 says God *asah*-created the firmament. It's not the same as in, say, *"Let there be light."* In this case, He really does sound more like an architect giving an assignment: "I want a firmament in between the waters. I want it to divide them up and keep them separate. I want some above and some below." The result: The earth now has (or will have) a distinct, and rather drier sky, with clouds and rain and gathered liquid waters below. It's no longer to be a steamy boiling mess. The verse then ends telling us *hayah,* "and it was (or became) so." This is not going to be the last time we see this pattern.

In verse 9 it appears the plan is carried on to the next step. And it's very interesting to discover exactly what the Scripture says about how it happens. The picture is quite dramatic—and full of remarkable details.

> Genesis 1:9 *And God said, Let the waters under the heaven be gathered together unto one place, and let the dry land appear: and it was so.*

Notice, first, that God said "land," not "lands." Notice, also, that He said the waters under the heaven should *"be gathered into one place."* Scientists now believe that's exactly the way the earth looked and exactly the way things happened long, long ago. It appears Moses got it right some 3500 years ago, well ahead of the researchers of today.

Scientists now believe that there was once but one land, one continent. And even today all the seas and oceans are still only one sea. All the waters, except for those captured temporarily in lakes, are still gathered into one place. The many oceans we call by different names and think of as separate are actually only one body of water. There may be many names, such as Atlantic Ocean and Pacific Ocean, but they are just different regions of that one sea. That's why you can sail around the world but not walk around it.

You can't drive or walk around the world, however, because there are many continents, which are now completely (well, partially) separated like big islands in that one sea. And no one, for a long time, ever suspected it wasn't always that way. Only in recent times when the scientists and map makers accumulated enough knowledge (from soil and geological data and satellite views of the earth) did they discover that all the continents, such as Africa and South America, are pieces broken apart from an original one.

Here's another little science lesson for you to help you get the picture and explain it to your children. It's really a lesson in "plate tectonic theory"! Be impressed!

Take a cookie, a large chocolate chip cookie is best, I think. Lay it on a dinner plate. That's our first original continent, the "land." OK, now break the cookie into five or six pieces. Shake and rattle it a little, just enough to crumble away the edges and create some little crumbs (for islands). Now put it back together again as best you can in the center of the plate. Now we can start the lesson in plate tectonics. Sliding the pieces apart, you have a picture of plate tectonics in action and the natural history of the earth, as if viewed from a satellite—assuming the scientists are right. Now spread the cookie pieces out to fill in the whole plate (maybe leave them a bit unevenly spread, letting two represent North and South America, and a few stand for Eurasia). And don't rotate them too much. Done? What you have is pretty close to what the earth looks like to the map maker and scientist. You'd have to scotch tape them on a beach ball to get any more realistic, and that's too hard!

If you look closely, you can even see some "clues" similar to those scientists have used to prove their theories. You might see a chocolate chip on the edge of one piece that matches a chocolate chip hole (maybe even with some chocolate left in it) on another. That's like the "geological evidence" that shows how western Africa and eastern South America were attached. See how easy this science stuff is?

Want to continue? Then move your cookie pieces around just a little bit. That's how our continents still move around. They "drift," literally floating around on the magma (melted liquid rock) core of the earth, somewhat as if on the surface of a water balloon. Continents move very slowly. Scientists measure it constantly, and you and I feel it occasionally. Even at only inches per year, they're still banging into each other fast enough to cause earthquakes, make mountains, create cracks and tears for volcanoes to push through, and tilt the coasts into or out of the level sea. Sometimes they even break, fold, or squeeze into wrinkles, giving us ocean bottoms in the sky or old forests and river channels under the sea.

These are the theories which your children learn in school and which are often exhibited as proof the Bible is out-dated and untrue. Yet we've just seen, as in verse 9, there is no necessary contradiction of the Bible. Instead, in the way we've read it, the Bible remains a remarkable picture written millennia before any mortal human should have known any such facts.

As we saw, verse 9 said there was initially but one continent formed, surrounded by one sea. Was it a mere accident or coincidence of language? It could have been, but before this book is done, we will have quite a long list of similar coincidences, if that's what they are. Was it, as I've heard suggested, an example of the ignorance of a desert-bound (fiction) writer who never dreamed there were other continents? If it was that, then we need to explain later Scriptures that show the Bible was quite aware of other lands—and even the breaking up of the original one! Genesis 10:25 rather quietly, without any fanfare, remarks: *"Two sons were born to Eber: One was named Peleg, because in his time the earth was divided."* We don't know whether this Scripture is telling us Peleg lived when the continents broke apart—some authorities argue Peleg lived much later, when the seas rose and separated Alaska and Siberia, for instance—but it is clear the writer was aware the land was broken apart.

Now let's look at something else that is quite remarkable about verse 9. We need to look closely at the Creation verbs. Recall, again, how the verse read.

> Genesis 1:9 *And God said, Let the waters under the heaven be gathered together unto one place, and let the dry land appear: and it was so.*

You might guess that the "Let the [waters] be . . ." is translated from our familiar *hayah,* but it is not. Another word, even more intriguing and scientifically surprising, was used in the Hebrew. The word is *qavah* ("kaw vaw"). The word carries the sense "collecting" or "gathering together," but it also says you wait for this to happen. It is used to express patience and hope as things come together or come to pass. This verse says that the waters aren't coming together immediately, but as we wait, we may confidently expect them to eventually gather into one place.

Some readers might have expected the Scriptures to say something such as "God gathered the waters together." After all, that is the powerful direct action thing a mighty god would do in a mere "creation story." The Scriptures, however, tell us He simply said, "Look! This is what's going to happen. . . ." It's as much an announcement as a command. And what is going to happen? Well the waters (those shallow waste waters covering the planet in verse 1) shall recede and gather into one place, a permanent place. Then a dry land shall rise and be seen.

The language used to say *"Let the [dry land] appear"* repeats that same sense—that we should not expect an instantaneous event, but a time-consuming process that should be watched with patience and expectation. The Hebrew uses *ra-ah,* which translates as "wait," or "watch for and observe." It will be a long process, indeed, if we believe the modern scientific version of the history of the world is anywhere near correct, and we think God used the "normal" processes of geology and plate tectonics. The forces inherent in a restless sphere of magma, pulled and squeezed by thermal and gravitational forces in the ponderous drift of the great continental plates surely could drain the immense supplies of water, which the Scriptures tell us were covering the whole earth surface, but it will be a long process indeed. But it will not be contradictory to the Genesis account: Wait. Watch. All those waters are going to gather together. Pay close attention, and you'll get to see the dry land appear.

This verse, after having given us so many clues that this was a long-term process (the sorting out of land and sea) ends with another little twist that seems to reinforce our idea that this "let the waters recede and the land appear" is an announcement of a long involved plan. That it is going to take some time to come to fruition. We have our familiar *hayah,* but it is conjoined with an adverb *ken* (" kane"), which changes the meaning somewhat. Instead of the more common "it came to be," or "happened thus," it extends the meaning a bit, and tells us "it happened in just that way" or "it came to pass just so."

That's as far as we'll go in this chapter. In the next, we'll begin to take up the origins of life on this planet. That's when it really gets interesting!

CHAPTER THREE

LET THE EARTH BRING FORTH . . . LIFE

Genesis 1:11 *And God said, Let the earth bring forth grass, the herb yielding seed, and the fruit tree yielding fruit after his kind, whose seed is in itself, upon the earth: and it was so.*

It's not a very big verse, but let me tell you, there's a lot going on in it. To set the background and give you a more intuitive sense of all that is going on in verse 11, let me take you through a little exercise in imagination. Let's create a little story, something like a parable. You get to be in it.

Imagine yourself being hired by an extremely rich man. Better yet, imagine you are being hired by a very large corporation, and he is about to become its new president and CEO. As part of his "perks," the corporation is going to give him an immense estate. They want this thing, this estate, to be so incredible that it will be the envy of even kings and sheiks. They have already built the new home, a palatial mansion, for him and his family. Now they are giving you unlimited resources—money, help, anything you want—to prepare the grounds and all its environment, to make it as grand and lavish a setting as you've ever seen. In fact, they want it to be better than anything you've ever seen before.

Though all the necessary buildings have been finished, they are standing on absolutely barren ground. The land has been stripped, bulldozed clear. It is empty. It is lifeless. You must create the rest of this estate from ground zero, from the first blade of grass to the last rose garden, from strawberry bed to apple orchard, from fish in the pond to pheasant in the field, from a canary in a cage to horses in the stable. It's up to you to make it a great place to live, to provide everything and anything the new family might want, need, or enjoy. You just have to have it all in place, and finished, when they arrive.

Have you put yourself into the story? Now imagine yourself standing just outside the house, surveying the barren grounds. You might wonder, briefly, who built the house, shops, stables, and barns, and who shaped the ground that you're now commissioned to turn into lawns, gardens, pastures, and orchards. Who sculpted ponds and channeled a stream; who decided where to leave hills and valleys. It has a rugged beauty, to be sure, but oh how silent and lifeless it is. There's a sadness in it. Loneliness. It literally cries out for the beauty and drama that only the panorama of life can provide. Without life, it's even, would you say, meaningless? You certainly have your work cut out for you!

You might begin with the ponds and stream. Do you put in lily pads or watercress? If you put in fish, what do they eat? Do you need to supply insects and tadpoles and whatever fish need to eat? What do the insects and tadpoles eat? Do you need to put in algae or something? Remember this place is absolutely barren. You need to put a whole ecology in place or it falls apart. Living things all fit together into a system, and you have to design and build that system.

Do you want to plant lawns and gardens? Put lots of flowers by the edge of the water? You'll need plenty of topsoil, because, except for a few plants like lichen, everything needs tons of "planter mix"!

Picture the pastures there, next to the stables. They need topsoil too. Nothing grows on plain rock, or gravel, or even sterile sand. And what about different kinds of grasses? Aren't pasture grasses of a special kind?

Design a walking path that meanders past the ponds and over the stream and takes them through endless varieties of flowers and trees. There definitely needs to be a grape arbor! And surely, you should plan for a variety of other fruits to be at hand, so they are available throughout all the seasons, or at least spring, summer, and fall. After all, what greater pleasure is there for one strolling the grounds than to be able to pick fruits in any season? This is not going to be easy, is it?

Our story—your imaginary job—of course, reflects about where we are in the Creation account. The groundwork is done; the future home of dry land and sea is built. But it is a barren and lifeless place. I often wonder what the young earth was like, at the end of verse 10. Or, if the "becoming," which the verse spoke of, stretched through some large amount of time, what was the earth like at the beginning of verse 11? Was it harsh and craggy, hard and bare? Or had the forces of time and erosion already done some of the work, smoothing and softening the "dry land" and grinding out the vital sands that give us beaches and dunes and, with the right mix of organic stuff, soil?

Was the earth still cold and barren like the Antarctic? Or was it hot and windswept like a desert in North Africa? What sort of climate could there be without the contribution which trees, grasses, and all the plant ecology make? They give us oxygen, humidity, cooling, hold the sands in place, and build up greenhouse gasses; the "system" is so interdependent and so creative in and of itself!

"Hey Mom, What About Dinosaurs?"

Was earth, perhaps, like the Mars landscape we saw recently through the camera eyes of Rover, NASA's little robot lander? Was it every bit as uninviting as that?

Now, that view of Mars we got a year or two ago was exciting, but it wore thin, didn't it? I don't know about you, but I was almost hoping to see a plant, or some creature come wandering into the picture. After a while, it actually became boring; so much "nothingness."

You know, we like to visit barren places like the north rim of the Grand Canyon, the ashen slopes of Mt. St. Helens, or the white sand deserts of New Mexico. But we stay only briefly. We never want to live there. We are creatures of life, and we always seek out the company of other life. There's undeniable comfort, and probably a sort of companionship, in both plants and animals. We want to see a lizard, a squirrel, or a deer at our campground. We even fill our house in the city with more plants and pets. It's a part of the design of all life, including ourselves, so the Genesis account tells us. And that design of all life and living things starts in verse 11.

> Genesis 1:11 *And God said, Let the earth bring forth grass, the herb yielding seed, and the fruit tree yielding fruit after his kind, whose seed is in itself, upon the earth: and it was so.*

At first glance, the designing of life in this is not all that obvious. In fact, there is much in that verse that is not obvious to a casual reading, or in the current translation. Most of us are casual readers, of course, and settle for the current translations. We aren't scientists, or particularly scholarly in our reading, and we don't really look all that closely at every bit of detail. We tend to see, in verse 11, merely that God created the plants. Just plants. But looking at it that way, we surely miss the answers we need when science, teachers, and our children come speaking doubts and asking the questions that unsettle our belief in Genesis.

I have one more story to tell before we get on with verse 11. I'm reminded of a relative who always amazed me. We'd go to museums and special collections from places like China and Dresden. I would go in and, even though I'm an absolute amateur about art and such things, I still took hours to get through it all. I could spend a quarter of an hour studying the artwork inscribed on a medieval suit of armor. It told the family history of the man who wore it. I could spend even longer examining the faces and clothing of the patrons in a painting of a restaurant in ancient China, painted over two thousand years ago. I would almost put myself into the life and scene portrayed there.

Meanwhile, my relative cruised the whole exhibit in a quarter of an hour and then waited patiently outside the exit. When I later quizzed him, I found he saw almost as much as I did. He saw all the items; even noted the engraving on the armor and how complete the Chinese village scene was. He might have missed some details—what was on the plates, what were the people wearing and doing—but he saw most of it. "Enough," he always said. And what is "enough"? It depends on what you want to get out of it. He "saw" it all, or most of it, but he missed the story. He was a bit like the listeners who never understood one of Jesus' parables, who never got the actual message. He didn't share the experience the artist was giving him. When he left the museum, he'd seen things, but he was never changed by them. He never heard the story the artist tried to tell, and even preserved for future generations.

That's what happens to most of us, most of the time, when we read the Bible. We especially tend to streak through the Old Testament. We don't immerse ourselves into the scene and the story as the ancient writer intended. Thinking we've seen enough, we miss the real story.

One other thing gets involved too. For some people "old" means "passè," not worth serious attention. For me, the very antiquity of the paintings and suits of armor was a big part of what impressed me so. I saw it as good reason to believe that what they showed was real history, that what was told was told with authority. It was better than some recent book by a historian 2000 years later. The Dresden armor, decorated with scenes of the owner's family history, kept his story (history) alive. The people in the Chinese restaurant were probably the neighbors of the artist, eating their fish, chatting and sharing their lives him about the same time Jesus was eating fish with Peter. I could almost be there, because I believed the artist painted the mealtime experience with authority. He was there!

Genesis comes to us claiming a similar authority. We know that the written text has an established 3500 years of antiquity. And we know that it is the first, and really the only, account that is not plainly fanciful imaginations (such as those full of dragons, planet-sized bird-snakes, or turtle-creators, etc.), which claims to be describing the history of Creation. Obviously, one can doubt or question the authenticity or authority of that claim. But as you follow through the rest of this work, I think I'll show you some very good scientific evidence to back up and substantiate Genesis' claim. I think that as we discover the accuracy, precision, and truth of various insights into the nature of living organisms, we can believe the Author was there!

When we read Genesis 1:11, even carefully, we common folk will probably miss the point that often starts scientists, even those ten and twelve year-old scientists in our families, right off down the path toward skepticism, toward believing there is little or nothing of merit in the Genesis Creation account. And what is it that raises such doubt? Well, it's another one of those little details, a seemingly small matter to a nonscientist, which includes most translators.

Look at verse 11 again.

Genesis 1:11 *And God said, Let the earth bring forth grass, the herb yielding seed, and the fruit tree yielding fruit after his kind, whose seed is in itself, upon the earth: and it was so.*

Look at that first phrase, *"Let the earth bring forth grass...."* To the scientifically knowledgeable, no matter how young, this is the first problem. Scientists believe, and make a pretty good case for it, that the first life to appear on the earth was of the single-cell (not "simple" cell—the simplest cell alive is more complex than your computer (and alive) type. It was pretty certainly "plant," but not a plant like you and I ordinarily think of when we think plant with roots, stems, and leaves. The first plants were single-cell individuals, possibly "loners," or maybe more like "herd plants," flocking together like algae scum. This is what the scientists believe, so they immediately conclude that the Bible has seriously missed the mark.

Grass, you see, is a fairly complex plant and quite a latecomer in the fossil record. Just one blade of grass (that is, not even including the root or flower and seed stalk) is millions of cells, of different types and various purposes, all very specialized, very organized, and very put together. A simple leaf of grass is something like a complex city of cells. There are cells that build a skeleton to hold everything up and in place; cells that transport in raw materials, such as water and chemical nutrients; cells that manufacture food; cells that expel waste; to mention just a few. They all do their own specific jobs together with an efficiency of organization and communication that puts most any human social structure to shame. So you see, grass is not "simple," but very complex, a rather "high" life form. And it doesn't show up in geological and fossil records until fairly late, probably later than dinosaurs in the history of life. In the evolutionary model we talked about in Chapter One, grass is not a square, but much more up the scale of complexity, like a hexagon.

Well, the truth is, the Bible agrees with the scientists! The Scripture, in the original language, doesn't say that grass came first, either. The Bible says about the same thing as the scientists (though doesn't give any time scale, such as "400 million years ago," as scientists do). The original Hebrew word, which the King James committee of scholars translated "grass," is *deshe*. Translating the word as "grass" is a simplification of the text and a rather poor and unfortunate selection of just one of the many things *deshe* can refer to. Just as "powder" is not the only kind of "snow" there is, and "sparrow" is not the only flying creature on earth, grass is not the only thing that grows green.

Had the King James translators known it was going to be important someday, they could have pointed out that the Hebrew word *deshe* also means any vegetation, any green plant life. In fact, "greenness," the most notable quality of plant life to the Hebrew mind, is the heart and essence of what *deshe* means. If the Hebrews had a word for chlorophyll, most likely *deshe* would be it. But once again, remind yourself that all this precise detail would have made for a rather messy translation or unwieldy footnote, and few readers of Genesis 1:11 could have appreciated the extra accuracy. In fact, they probably would not have appreciated it at all. Keeping in mind the culture of England and the royal house in which the King James committee was serving, how do you think it would have gone over translating verse 11 as, "And God said, let the earth bring forth algae (or scum)"? Probably not well, huh? So their translation of *deshe* is no surprise, nor indictment of their scholarship. It's just good that we can correct it now.

I hope you share my pleasure in what we find here. I find this new sort of insight and understanding of the Scripture and evidence for the true precision and accuracy of the Genesis account downright exciting. I'm even more delighted to see how it not only disarms that major scientific criticism but how it actually stands confirmed by the latest evidence in science.

Here's something else you might appreciate. Scum, which is how algae often appears to our untrained eye, can itself be seen as something quite beautiful and glorious, once you understand how complex and miraculous a thing even one algae cell is. Let's look at it a little more closely. Look at it under a microscope. In just a single cell, you'll discover a veritable little "village" of cell-part actors carrying on the incredible miracle of life within its walls. Hundreds of biochemical cell-part "citizens" are bustling about in the commerce of life. Now increase your magnification level a few thousand-fold, using an electron microscope perhaps, to a point where you can reveal the atoms. Try to map its atoms and molecules. They look like an almost infinite set of intricately assembled "tinker toys" (millions of them!) far more complicated than anything you could ever put together. Beyond what you could even draw as a map, a blueprint, or schematic chart. A single little plant cell, an infinitesimal speck of an algae scum, dwarfs anything mankind has assembled.

So you see, the simplest version of life is already incredibly complex. No one has ever "built" a cell, even with all our modem technology. Not even come close. And it's still another quantum leap, from the mechanical (say, chemical) level of "building" or "assembling" a cell-like structure, to the supernatural level of life—that is, to get any such assemblage of parts to actually become "alive." However outrageously complex a structure that simplest algae cell is, what truly makes it special is something that seems to be outside and above the million atoms and intricate structure—it lives. You can even take away bits and pieces of it, within limits, of course, and it still does what no other structure of atoms, molecules, pieces of rock, metal, or you name it, does. It lives. It reproduces and it recreates itself. Again and again and again. It took a dazzling miracle and a very incredible Creator, to produce just that first awesome bit of *deshe*. It's very hard to imagine it happening by accident. It certainly hasn't happened by design and effort yet. In spite of centuries of effort, scientists have not been able to create anything near a new speck of life in a laboratory.

Well, that's the whole and true story told in that first act of Creation in Genesis 1:11. It actually told about the simplest and most elementary plant life, *deshe,* a fact well in accord with the scientific view of the order of Creation, and yet it was one most incredible, almost impossible, feats of Creation—another fact well in accord with scientific experience. Critics, who have assumed the Scripture here was false, or falsifiable, were wrong. They simply hadn't really read the Scripture accurately.

By the way, algae is not the only plant that should be thought of as *deshe*. In the economy of language in Genesis, *deshe* can reasonably stand for many simple plant life forms, algae being only one of the simpler and better known. Mosses and ferns, and perhaps even fungi, lichen, and such should be included. With only three categories being used, each covers a lot of specific plants.

The second part of Genesis 1:11 reads, *"the herb yielding seed. . . ."* We can regard this second phrase as the second major act of Creation, of plant life, anyway. Remember, putting both phrases into one verse was an editorial choice made by a printer about 1550 A.D. and does not truly reflect anything in the original Hebrew writing. This second phrase, *"the herb yielding seed,"* could just as easily been set apart and numbered verse 12. If it had been, it would have pointed out more clearly that this second phrase is spelling out a second category of plants and a second category of Creation. And when the Scripture does specify a second distinct type of plants as it does here, it gives a pretty strong confirmation of the interpretation we just made—that *deshe* is about the lower non-grass types of plants. How so?

First, "herb yielding seed" is exactly what grass is, botanically. Furthermore, *eseb* is the Hebrew word being translated "herb" here, and *eseb* is commonly used for "grass" throughout all the Scriptures.

Second, the fact we first have *deshe,* and then we are next told God created *eseb,* certainly suggests grass was not supposed to be included in, or considered as, the first stuff created.

I think we must trust that God is careful and precise and intended the Creation account to be the same. Any blurring of the meanings and categories that makes Genesis look to be in error is surely due to our own poor translating and comprehension, not His error.

So we see again, in the second phrase, that the original language of Genesis is not contradicted by what scientists have deduced but is only confirmed! Simple plant life was indeed the first life to appear. Not grass. Grass, along with the other seed-producing plants, is the second level of Creation. So what about the third phrase and the third category of plants it specifies?

The third category is *"the fruit tree yielding fruit."* "The . . . tree" is translated from *ets,* (pronounced "ates"), which is a Hebrew word for a whole category of plants that are "firm" (the Hebrew language pays close attention to aspects of motion), having woody stalks and stems. That is, in itself, a next higher level of plant and appears later than the first two in the fossil record. But here in the Scripture, it is also specified that these are those trees, shrubs, and vines that yield fruit. The fruit-bearing species, which are botanically classified the highest level of plants, are also the last to appear in the scientists' now accepted version of the fossil record. Are we surprised to find that the Bible sets it forth just as science now sees it?

So, in just this one verse, Genesis 1:11, the Bible gives its entire outline of the plants, which I am sure is also telling us the order of their creation. If we accept verse 11 thusly, as an outline and indication of order, it pairs up quite well alongside the scientific botanical classification hierarchy and the fossil record, both of which are used to justify the evolutionists' idea of the history of plant kingdom origins.

But we must always keep this in mind: The Genesis Creation account is only an outline. Genesis gives only the briefest sketch, with very few details. Remarkably accurate, perhaps, but still very brief. It's definitely an outline, not a textbook. As such, Genesis says very little about how God created or about how He brought things into being. It also tells us little about the "inner nature" or principles and laws of life as a good biology text would try to do. But don't think Genesis tells us nothing. As usual, we just need to set aside the traditional translations, which ignore or disdain "scientific" issues, and analyze the originals from the Hebrew.

Then we discover these Scriptures, however brief and cryptic they might be, still give us some extraordinary hints and clues about the nature of life and about the principles that life-processes follow. In fact, with hindsight, and with the knowledge we have from science today, these subtle clues are often far from subtle; they're more like blaring headlines! And some of them can be translated into veritable pages of information. It sometimes seems as if the Bible has been teasing us along a path of discovery like a parent helping a little child along in an Easter egg hunt. Or, as if it is actually daring us, with all our scientific prowess, to find the truth. And once we find the truth and understanding it was pointing to, shouldn't we wonder how that ancient manuscript could have "known"?

To tell you the truth, I tend to take this idea a bit further. I tend to see the Genesis Creation account much the same as prophecy!

LET THE EARTH BRING FORTH . . . LIFE

I see it as giving numerous prophetic signs, or "signposts," that should, as prophecy does, point us toward the Creator—for only He could possibly know so much of the end from the beginning.

Prophecy, of course, tells us about something we will experience at a future time. The signposts in Genesis were placed at least 3500 years ago; what they point to (the future "events" they predict in this case) is knowledge. Only now are scientists, even if working from different theoretical premises, finally uncovering—or constructing—the story about how and when (or in what order) the various forms of life appeared. And it turns out that the story is exactly what the Scriptures have described 3500 years before there was any "science." That looks very much like prediction, or prophecy, to me. Of course, even when the Bible proves it is absolutely "right on" about such matters the determined nonbeliever can always disregard it, calling it chance, lucky guess, or coincidence. They may even accuse us of stretching it with our new translations. But for those of us who are more open-minded, whether certain or uncertain in our beliefs, the signposts we find in Genesis should carry some weight.

We might have something we can call a signpost in the first phrase of verse 11, *"let the earth bring forth the deshe."* As we've seen, the three-part list of plant life types begins with the simplest and lowest plants and with the first in the history of life's origins, the algae, mosses, etc. These are all water borne, or very water-dependent, life forms. They are all stagnant water or marshy plants. This is a bit contrary to what we might expect. No sooner have the Scriptures announced that the "dry land" was being readied for verse 11, than we go to the very wet areas, even marshy waters, to create plants. And, essentially announce that this is where it first began. Not only does verse 11 tell us that, you'll find it repeats the message more explicitly when we get to animal life! That is an accuracy that almost rises to the level of signpost to me.

There is nothing obvious about the idea that life arose in the marshy waters of early Earth. It certainly shouldn't have been obvious to a desert-dwelling people like the ancient Hebrews. It wasn't obvious to scientists until about the early 1800's. Since that time, however, scientists have been pretty unanimous in their belief that it did. How, they still don't know, but they are quite sure it happened in a swampy (algae's favorite home) environment.

How the first instance of life, the very first living something, came to be available for evolution to start working on, is a big threshold problem for the anti-Creator folks. Lots of Dr. Frankenstein-types have spent tons of time and money trying to get life to pop up out of mucky ooze. Using artificial lightening, cooking it, mixing up countless recipes of special "enriched" mud, they've tried every which way but successful to get it to "just happen."

In recent times they've adjusted their theory a little. One reason, of course, is they finally figured out that true swamp muck itself is a mix of mud and now dead (so, already previously living) organic stuff. The earlier experiments were more or less just trying to "jump-start" some dead squares (those simplest life forms in our evolution model of Chapter One) back into living. Now they're trying to get some organic stuff to come up out of the ooze a bit more honestly, not just from the remains of once-living things. They know the real problem is to get not just a square to come together, but to get a bunch of dots to line up into straight lines, and for those to pull themselves together into a real, perfect living square. Most modern experiments are using certain kinds of clay they think would have been lying around and could have made various chemicals pull off that sort of feat. All that is quite a bit beyond our scope here, but the interesting point is that while they increase their understanding of the problem of imitating that life/creation/threshold, they are also increasing their certainty that it had to start in the marshy waters! Now take my word for it, the new theories and experiments haven't worked either. Haven't come close. But, it's interesting to note that the harder they try, and the more clever they get trying to match the Creator, the closer they come to the pointer of the signpost in Genesis: "Let the earth bring forth *deshe.*"

There's another signpost in verse 11 that points to a lot of what we're now discovering about the nature of the life He created. It's found in the remainder of the verse, *"the herb yielding seed and the fruit tree yielding fruit after his kind whose seed is in itself."* The key is in the words "seed" and "kind."

Zera is the word translated "seed." We all know what a seed is, and so did men thousands of years ago. Right? Well, almost right. Until a century or so ago, we knew what seed did, the purpose of it—to faithfully produce its own "kind" generation after generation—but we weren't at all informed about how and why, and we weren't sure how faithful and accurate it was. A lot of science went on trying to get seed to not produce faithfully and true.

Verse 11 says these are plants that scatter or sow their own *zera,* and the Hebrew language says *zera* is the "offspring," the "posterity," of those plants. It also says that this *zera* is *miyn,* "after his (its) own kind." *Miyn* adds an important property to fully explain and describe *zera.* Both the herbs (all complex leafy plants) yielding just seeds, and the trees (all woody plants) yielding fruits, have a seed within themselves that reproduces each kind *"after his kind."* You might call it "The Law of Conservation." Or you might call it "The Law of Genetics." *Miyn* declares that in the seed (*zera*) and the fruit (this is made even more exact and explicit in the restatement of verse 12), there is not just any "offspring" or "descendants," but "only its kind of offspring," "only its type (species, genus, or biological type) of descendants." The signpost is clearly pointing to workings of genetics.

For many centuries, men believed in the power of *zera miyn;* that seed would reproduce true to its own kind. They didn't know why it did, but they believed it. The rise of evolutionary theories, including Darwin's, came after a century of doubt, after a time when men believed that if we changed the plant or its environment, we could change the seed and produce new "kinds." They were trying to compose a sort of "we can do it," or "Mother Nature does it," theory of creation. Darwin's theory of evolution (descent with modification) developed in a time when scientists were beginning to have more confidence in the idea of *zera* but still not believing in *miyn*. They thought that the conservative rule God applied within the reproductive principle of *zera* was flawed, and it somehow slipped up once in a while, letting out new "kinds"—a sort of "oops" creation theory. Of course, all of the above theories involved replacing God as the Creator. They are all no-God creation theories.

Looking only at the scientific thinking (and ignoring the theological bias—atheism), we can trace much of Evolutionism to success in animal and plant husbandry, selective breeding. We'd had a long history of success in breeding new (better?) breeds of sheep, dogs, or whatever. Though they were never new "kinds," or species, but only races or varieties, hopeful evolutionists, both before Darwin and since, deduced from this success in breeding new breeds (technically, subspecies) that a new species could eventually be made, "evolved" (by us, or by Mother Nature). It was just a matter of degree.

All this time we didn't know about DNA and the incredible power and precision of its constructive message—the power of *zera*. Nor, of course, did we know of conservative strength, the ability to resist change, built into the DNA message system—the power of *miyn*. Of course, once we did, the evolutionists modified Darwinism into neo-Darwinism (same theory incorporating the scientific facts of genetics) and kept on going undaunted for about thirty more years and are, only now, stumbling as the *zera* and *miyn* principles of DNA start becoming a little more obvious and hold their own.

Let me explain a little about DNA, the modern scientific name for the mechanism and process of *zera* seed, and genetics, the modern scientific study of *miyn* and *zera* together.

Most of you probably have some idea of what DNA (and genes and chromosomes) is. But you probably don't have a very good idea of just how powerful it is. DNA, you see, is a coded string of molecules, much like a written language is a coded string of characters (such as the alphabet), or as a computer file or instruction is a coded string of electronic characters (such as bits). Our alphabet is made up of twenty-six characters and with it we can encode an infinite variety of information. Your computer uses two characters to do the same thing. Genes use four characters. They encode (almost) every bit of the information that builds, directs, operates, and maintains every living cell. Even the simplest cell, say our algae cell, has a string of DNA information that dwarfs what's in your home library. Essentially, every cell in your body has a string of DNA six feet long (!), made up of an atom-sized "alphabet." In that six-foot string is more information than in all the encyclopedia sets ever published.

DNA is, essentially, a chemical, or biochemical, a computer system, hardware and software together. The information it packs is carried in a CD-ROM fashion—to be read only, no rewriting allowed. That CD-ROM aspect is a big part of how the *miyn* system works. But, in one of the most unfathomable "mysteries" of life (one of the real "miracles" of a cell's life), this CD can periodically make a complete copy of itself, a total backup copy of all files; all while it is facilitating (or inspiring) the simultaneous assembling of the essentials of another cell in which it will put the new CD-ROM. That's a wee bit like finding your computer automatically manufacturing (from raw earth materials) a new computer right there on your desk, filling it with software, powering it up, and setting it to working! (That's almost scary!) Just about every living thing (every cell), even every living cell in every multi-cellular "community" that we recognize as a higher plant or animal does that DNA and "reproduction" thing! Regularly. Periodically. Since the beginning, since the first cell was. There are a few exceptions, but were we to bother discussing them here, they would only add to the sum of miracles in this living DNA story.

That sure gives you a new insight into the Old Testament meaning of seed, as in "Abraham's seed," doesn't it? God said the seed of nations was in him. Well, every person that every lived, who is a descendent of Abraham, carries some of his genetic seed. If Adam and Eve were what the Scriptures say, the first mother and father of us all, then we should have their genes, right? Some very interesting research, by the way, tracking genes and the various varieties or variations designed into the system, has attempted to calculate: 1) if Eve lived, 2) where she lived, and 3) when she lived. They have come up with some very interesting results (including the conclusion that there was an Eve!)—and have really irritated those who never wanted to know.

Most scientists, even Evolutionists, probably see little to disagree or argue with in what we just discussed. They certainly know that DNA (which they only discovered in the 1950's) is very much a *zera* and *miyn* kind of stuff. But they do have to take issue with the real "law" part of it, the "Law of Conservation," enforced by *miyn,* because *miyn* says no to evolution. *Miyn,* when applied to a "kind" (whether that be a species or a higher grouping of animal or plant varieties), says that each and every member of the kind not only carries within itself its own *zera,* but that it also shall remain true to itself, reproducing only the same "kind," or the same species. Now that denies evolution absolutely, at least at the "kind" level. A rose shall beget a rose that shall beget a rose. *Miyn* doesn't say that all roses shall be exact copies, without individuality or races (varieties), unchangeable in time, unable to change to adjust to its particular environment. To the contrary, *miyn* applies to populations, to the level of "kind," just as the sciences of genetics and population genetics understand it does. That's exactly why selective breeding can happen. *Miyn* only says that all descendants of the rose, however varied or adapted (and the Jews full well knew husbandry and selective breeding), shall yet be roses.

That does not deny validity to the concept of evolution, per se, because we do not know for certain what a "kind" is. It used to be thought that it was a species, whatever that is (scientists now have about fifteen significantly different definitions of species). It might mean genus, though the definition of a genus, and what varieties belong in which genus, is widely disputed. Whatever the precise referent of "kind" is, it still does deny the hope and concept of evolution that Evolutionists have. Why? Because there's no denial of individual and population (racial) differences in *miyn*. But Genesis explicitly says that every "kind" is created only by God's authority and design and *miyn* absolutely applies.

The Bible was well aware of hybridization, animal husbandry, and selective breeding. They are referred to many times. They may well even function as the source of the "new shapes" we think are new species (wholly new *zera* and new exclusive *miyn*). This is all about micro-evolution, something we (well, scientists and students) have observed and documented at lower than species level and at species level in the lowest levels of plants and animals. And we will soon discover that the Scriptures at least leave the door open to micro-evolution at those lower (i.e., category one in Genesis 1:11) levels. It may even be a part of the plan. We'll get to that shortly.

To sum it up, *miyn* says: "Variety, yes; flexibility and adaptability, yes; races, yes; new species, we're not sure; new kinds, not amongst the higher levels and not without His intention!"

"Hey Mom, What About Dinosaurs?"

Let me say a little more about *miyn*. It's about my own understanding of where and how some of the *miyn* power is embedded in the *zera*.

DNA contains a surprising lack of efficiency, or economy, from an information theory or engineering point of view. There is a lot of code that is repetitious. Perhaps a foot or two of your six feet of DNA are not necessary! It's like having several, if not thousands, of copies of the same program on your computer. That seems contrary to numerous laws of nature and logic. It even seems a contradiction of some fundamental principles and axioms in the evolutionary paradigm, including the ruthless grim reaper "natural selection," which says waste is dangerous and usually fatal, and that useless, non-functional "shapes" must perish before too long. Needless to say, many compensatory theories (rationalizations) are offered up to make it refit into evolutionary logic and other biological facts that they want DNA's characteristics to support.

Well, what do you think? Why should either evolutionary processes, or a Divine Designer, be so wasteful and inefficient as to repeat the same instructions when one would do? Why say "Produce protein A, or cell-part #286," a thousand times, when you only need one recipe for the protein or four recipes of part #286? In evolutionary terms, in good evolutionary theory, it is definitely wasteful. And evolution-via-natural-selection really is a theory of economics. It parallels a familiar business edict—the best product (species or variant) or the most economically produced product (no waste of energy or materials) will eventually win out in the market place (the environment). DNA redundancy is so contrary to such principles and rationale of evolutionary theory, it could be held up as another major refutation of the theory. But as a means to establish *miyn*, however, it may be simply a clever and effective design.

The redundancy of the DNA code, as a power of *miyn*, actually shows ŭp in two forms. In one, the same instructions, or recipes, may be repeated thousands of times. In another, there may be hundreds of small and rather insignificant, but possibly helpful, variations of the same thing. Like a hundred different recipes that produce a chocolate chip cookie, or genetic instructions that supply hair color or bird beaks. Version A may be better in a certain situation than the other versions (No brand A chocolate chips in the store, or your guest is allergic to brown sugar, etc.). The first redundancy, exact repetition, means that errors, tampering, or mutations, can be muffled and drowned out, or simply over-ridden by redundancy, by the repetition of the correct instruction, i.e. 1000 good proteins and one bad one is no problem. Like the hometown fans drown out the puny cheers of the visiting cheerleaders. The other, repeated instructions with minor and non-harmful variations, allow helpful adjustments (adaptations) to different circumstances. That preserves the "kind" when the circumstances (environment) is not adequately preserved.

Darwin, in observing the many variations on the theme ("kind") of finches, thought he saw evolution, a set of creations without God's hand in it (so he assumed). When modern science discovered DNA, Darwinists thought they had discovered the means nature used to do the job (by mutations). They ignored two facts. One, when things go wrong (mutations), they are almost always tragic and never create some giant leap into a new kind. Two, *miyn* is well built into the DNA system and maintains the kinds, just as planned. Evolution, when God does not want it (as in the "after his kind" limitation applied to seed plants and trees of verse 11) is prohibited. If He doesn't mind and doesn't apply *miyn* to the *zera*, then maybe it can take place within the limits He sets.

Might such a situation ever exist? Well, let's take one more look at verse 11. If we look closely, we can see something surprising to many of us; it appears that *miyn* is not applied to *deshe!* Verse 11 doesn't explicitly apply it or deny it. But verse 12, which seems at first glance, to simply repeat the Creation outline given in verse 11, clearly omits to apply the rule of *miyn* to the *deshe,* the first levels of life. You might well miss that if you're reading the King James Version, because the translators obscured it by adding an unwarranted "and" (a common practice to make the text more readable) to the original Scripture. Verse 12 should read:

> Genesis 1:12 *And the earth brought forth [deshe]; [not "and"] . . . herb yielding seed after his kind, and the tree yielding fruit, whose seed was in itself, after his kind and God saw that it was good.*

Phrase "a," the first category, or level of life, is not connected with an "and" (remember, I said it could have stood as a separate verse the first time it was set forth), and has no *"after his kind."* Phrase "b," about herb yielding seed has its own *"after his kind";* and phrase "c" about trees with seeds is both joined to "b" and supplied with its own *"after his kind."* Does that mean that the lowest forms of life, like the single cell plants, might be mutable, or even evolve? That's a very important question with inestimable consequences—both for the scientists and us. Before this book is done, we will attempt to answer it. But first we must analyze a couple more verses that also bear on the question.

The next section of the Genesis Creation account, Creation-day four, takes a somewhat surprising turn. You might even think it is a U-turn. Since Genesis 1:2, we've been very much earthbound. Genesis 1:11 began creating life, and we have already worked through three levels of plants, in Creation-day three. Now, abruptly, Genesis 1:14 returns, so it appears, to account for another part of the greater physical universe.

> Genesis 1:14 *And God said, Let there be lights in the firmament of the heaven to divide the day from the night; and let them be for signs, and for seasons, and for days, and year.*

This verse looks to be completely out of place. Good writing, good story telling, even good textbook layout, follows some rather straightforward and obvious organizational principles. It's not in keeping with any of them to suddenly bounce us out of "the origins of life" and back into astronomy. It sure looks like an "oops, I forgot to mention something about the stars!" So I think we should approach this "bounce" with some wariness. We ought to presume that there is a good reason for it; that this out-of-place information is itself intended to tell us something. By now we should always assume there's nothing careless or accidental in Genesis 1, and there may often be as much information in the form and organization of the outline as there is in the content of the words themselves. This verse, I think, may bring that point home more than any other may.

So, what is it we may learn from this apparent detour in Genesis 1:14? The plain and obvious information, the linguistic content of the verse, is that God made the stars and constellations. That isn't a big surprise. That essentially follows from the first verse in the Scriptures, even if it wasn't explicitly said. But we are also told here that the arrangements of the stars and galaxies are not random or happenstance. God designed them. He planned and positioned them throughout the universe with our earthbound perspective and us in His mind, and for His purpose! Though the stars, galaxies, and other luminescent things are scattered throughout the unimaginable vast expanses of three (or four) dimensional space, He positioned them all (or certain ones of them), so that when we see their light in our skies—as they look to us, earthbound as we are—they appear as constellations or other signs. That's what the Bible says.

This is, by the way, the only time God explicitly tells us His "why" for doing something, in Genesis 1. We are told that He made (or arranged) the things in space, which appear as stars, to be worldwide (thus reaching all mankind) signs for storytelling and calendar keeping. That was a long time ago, before any men were even around. But let me assure you, anthropological studies have shown that the plan worked. Few, if any, of all the nations throughout the earth have forgotten, or ignored at least, those uses! Various peoples may have changed the stories associated with the signs, and often used them to mark a very different list of events in their celestial calendar, but they still used them. Surprisingly, often they used the same stars in the same groups for remarkably similar signs and stories. Anthropologists like to say that this is because of "cultural diffusion," i.e. the similarities have come about because ancient peoples have somehow bumped into each other at their tribal boundaries and shared their stories. Equally tenable, if you accept the biblical history, is the theory that the differences and variations we find are because of "drift," i.e. as tribes went their separate ways and invented new traditions and religions, they forgot or gradually changed the originals.

The calendar functions "for seasons, and for days, and for years," depend also on a curious design feature of earth, the tilt of the earth on its rotational axis. As the earth rotates, it precesses; it slowly rotates around a tilted axis just as a toy top does. Quite conveniently, it precesses a full circle each year, and the seasons and many other calendrical features, are much more clearly marked out than if it did not. (By the way, that precession is also very vital for creation-life supporting conditions on the earth!)

That's the obvious verbal content of the verse. But here is where I think there is additional information, a message written behind the obvious. I believe God also tells us, by this placement in verse 14, when He made the signs, which the stars form, appear in the earthly sky. That's the information encoded in the out-of-order appearance of the account. To begin with, we are told they appeared in Creation-day four, but that's only the first part of the "when" story.

He also tells us, by virtue of interrupting His account, and by indicating that this was after life had already begun appearing on earth, something very basic about the creation of the universe.

Remember that the Bible says that God "stretched out" the vast expanse of the universe at the very beginning? Well, the scientific evidence that leads the scientists to their "Big Bang" theory is information and data that very strongly suggests that the expansion of the brand new universe was extremely rapid. Far faster than a speeding bullet. Far faster, even, than a speeding ray of light (photon, technically). It was so fast, that if we were to see it from earth, we'd have considered it instantaneous. Like the airbag in a car. Now, obviously the universe is huge and very massive (heavy). So just like a speeding freight train, it didn't simply slam into a complete halt after He stretched it out. It had such great momentum, in fact, that it appears it still is expanding, though it is slowing down, and the light from way out there is now trickling back in. Remember the speed limit on light we discussed in Chapter Two? Well, it is taking the light from out there, a long time to get here. It's rather like we, on earth, can truly see the trailing edge of His glorious work.

But back when the "Big Whoosh" took place, that expansion of the universe was horrendously faster than light. There wasn't any light at all coming our way from all those other stars being stretched out and away from us. Or at least it wasn't coming fast enough our way, to overcome the "retreat," or "going away" of the light sources (our stars). The light (or any type of radiation, such as radio and x-ray) was being "sucked out" along with the stars themselves. If that picture eludes you, think of it like this: You walk forward toward the rear of a fast-moving train. To your feet and your mind, you are walking forward. To the earth and to me standing outside watching through the windows, you are going backward. If I were standing behind the train, watching you run toward me as fast as you could, you could not get to me as the train raced away. That's how the light of the stars was being "pulled" away from the earth, perhaps until they slowed down to less than the speed of light, and light could overcome the going-away, and make progress (at the speed of light) toward us.

In Creation-day four, the lights are finally arriving! And our Narrator knows that now we would notice them and pauses to tell us "By the way, I created those lights and arranged them to tell you things. . . ." Out of this extra bit of precision in the Creation account given to us earthbound listeners, comes clues about the timing and the size and the nature of the universe, if we will only listen carefully and accept His authority (as I did regarding my Chinese artist). Another possible explanation, by the way, of this timing of the constellations' appearance is that by this time of Creation-day four, interstellar space and our atmosphere had gotten clean enough that the faint (lesser) lights could be at last seen on the ground.

Whichever explanation we may choose to believe, I trust you can see, anyway, how the placement of this verse could be another of those signposts placed in Genesis.

Crucial to this last interpretation, and many others we make in this study, are some important assumptions about time. These are assumptions that many of us might not understand or might not be quite ready to agree with. So I'd like to take a brief break here and talk a little bit more about time.

If we really stop to think about it, most of us will confess that time is a confusing "something," at best. While we all share common terms and labels—minute, day, year, even past, future, and now—we all experience it in very individual ways. For some, time flies, for others it drags. Some days or events go fast, others never seem to end. The young usually cannot wait for life to move on; the old regret, the haste of years. You get the idea, don't you?

I've shared this idea of time with friends and find many agree with me. Time is a bit like being on an amusement park ride—say, a wild roller coaster—that we aren't always so sure we should have gotten on. We're stuck on it for the duration, and there's no way we can get off until it's over; it's totally out of our control. It's a one-way trip, and it's a different experience for everyone else on the ride! Some love it, some hate it, some get sick, and others are thrilled. Some lose their cameras, and so on.

I suspect that if we didn't have clocks and calendars, hardly any of us would agree with any one else very much about time! Ever try to meet someone, somewhere, who lost track of time or whose watch stopped? Try comparing your idea of how soon Christmas is coming to that of an eight-year-old child. How does your slow day at work compare to a friend's day at a business convention?

In science, time is very important and needs to be measured every bit as accurately as length and width and weight. Science is all about accurate measurement, and time is one of the major elements of everything that exists. So scientists must work with very accurate and very carefully shared concepts of time. Have you noticed how modern scientists can talk about nanoseconds and light-years without any apparent problems? I don't know about you, but most of us non-scientific-types just nod our heads, pretending we understand when we really haven't the foggiest idea of what either a light-year or a nanosecond is! We're satisfied to simply figure out Brand A computer is faster and better if it does something in one nanosecond instead of twenty like Brand X does. It's better for something, anyway, isn't it?

And aren't light-years supposed to mean a distance? When they talk about the Creation of the universe, light-years are both a time and distance measurement. Talking about the origins of plants, the theory of evolution, and such stuff, scientists talk about eras and ages that encompass millions and billions of years. Those sorts of terms make about as much real sense to us as it does when someone talks about the size of the US national debt. You and I live about threescore and ten (years) and earn a few million dollars in a lifetime, if we're lucky. Billion-year time scales and trillion-dollar debts are just a wee bit beyond our imagination. So how do we sensibly compare billion-year "evolution schemes" to the Genesis Creation outline? Especially when the Bible doesn't really say anything, or certainly not much, about time in the Genesis Creation account?

"Wait a minute," I can hear someone protesting, "it says 'six days!'" Of course, we read the word "day," in the six Creation-days of Genesis, and we know that the most traditional interpretation is that all of the Creation took place in six 24-hour days. The first man, Adam, came in Creation-day six; and a church bishop once calculated (in about 1650 A.D.), that Old Testament genealogies show that Creation-day six was a little over 6000 years ago. So do we have a time scale? If you think so, and if you think each of the Creation-days was a true twenty-four-hour day as we currently know them, and if you believe that the whole of Creation took place in one six-day, 144-hour week about 6000 years ago, then I ask to put those ideas on hold for a little while. Don't quit the belief just because I say so, but pretend you don't know it. OK? Let me take you through a little reasoning, a little logic, and a little deeper look into what "time" is, first. Then let me take you through a little deeper look into what the original Scriptures say. Then decide what you will about time and dates in creation.

We'll begin by looking at time from a "natural world" perspective, in a more-or-less scientific and technical way.

To start with, you should understand that time is just another natural dimension. You've heard that we live in four-dimensional space, right? Three of those dimensions are very "space" dimensions, as you and I usually think of things. Height, width, or depth is one way to label them. Each one is seen, directly experienced, and measured as some sort of "length." We usually feel pretty comfortable about them. We feel we know what they are and that everyone agrees with what we think they are. But even those three dimensions can be pretty subjective, a different sort of experience for each person. A "long way" is not the same thing for every one. A toddler or an arthritic person doesn't think of a mile the same way a jogger does.

To get around that problem, we establish a standard reference, a scale that everyone measures by. In the USA, these are kept in a government office, the Bureau of Standards. A foot, inch, and meter are all standards, intended to get around the subjective "feeling," and let even different societies know each other's language. An important part of our education, especially our scientific and technical training, involved learning what those standard measures are and how to use them. They are fundamental to civilization and technology. Try to imagine buying and selling without standards of money, weight, size, length, etc. Try laying out cities, building buildings, or drawing maps. Objective measurement is at the foundation and beginning of science and technology.

Time is the fourth dimension. Time is a little more difficult to understand than the other three. Remember how subjective time is to us non-scientific-types? If we each experience something as simple as a mile very personally, you can bet that time is going to be a lot more subjective than the other three dimensions. That's partly because we can't even "see" it. We can't mark it out with something like a stake in the ground, and we can't look back over time traveled and be sure our neighbor, or even our spouse, brother, or sister sees it the same way we do. Time is just tough stuff to deal with, probably harder than "happiness," "comfort," or "pretty."

Since time is invisible and rather immaterial (can't touch it), we essentially have to refer to something else when we want to talk about it. Throughout most of human history, we've referred to certain events. That can include worldly things, like moons, seasons, or other cyclical happenings. Personally, we often mark time by things like a birthday, a holiday, or past personal history. But as we get more technical and standardized, maybe we use a calendar, a tick of a clock, or even a vibration of a particular atom (as in your quartz watch). Without them, how could we even agree on what a second or an hour is? If we didn't have a clock in Greenwich and a worldwide treaty, how would you even precisely say when Thursday ended and Friday began?

Another terribly difficult thing about time for us all is that we only experience it exactly where we are, and only in a forward direction (that roller coaster ride). We can't go backward, sideways, or any way, but forward. We can only "remember" backwards. And though forward is completely invisible to us (as if we're on the roller coaster with our eyes closed), we still have no choice except to go forward at full speed. We can only guess at what is coming—which is one of the strongest incentives to trust the future to God, wouldn't you say? But why should we think He can help? Maybe it's because we believe He can see the end from the beginning, as the Scriptures promise, and as they try to prove to us through fulfilled prophecy. Maybe it's because we also just sense He isn't locked into that one (or one-half, actually) dimension of time as we are. Whoa! Did I just lose you, there? Well, let's try it from another angle.

You probably have read some science fiction or seen movies that have the theme of "time travel" in them. You know, the idea that people can go back in time, not just forward. Well, let's pretend for the moment, such time travel (or getting off the roller coaster of time) is possible for God and God's angels. Maybe you'll get the idea better if we substitute a skier's towrope for the roller coaster. Think of life as holding on to the towrope of time. You and I can't ever let go; we have to simply hold on until we reach the end.

If God's angels and assistants are not required to lock onto the one-half dimension of time that we are locked onto (our towrope), then a whole lot of the things His angels do seem a lot less supernatural. They could be really quite natural and easy for them. For instance, an angel could say "Hi" to you, as you're about to go into your house, then scoot back a little in time and go inside before you got there. Then he's in there to say "Hi" again when you go in! Suppose you're surrounded by an army. An angel comes and bobs in and out of your moment in time and shows himself hundreds of times in a ring around the army. They think they're surrounded by a whole host!

Besides that sort of thing, their abilities to come and go infinitely and instantly, forward and backward in time, mean they'd never need miss an appointment or fail to finish an assignment. They could build a brick wall, just while staying in the same moment in time, and it would look to you, a "normal" time traveler, like the wall just popped up! Those sorts of "miracles" could be explained by that one simple fact—they are not locked onto our limited dimension of time. They are free to be everywhere, anywhere, anytime, and every time.

There may be distance for Gabriel, but even the greatest distance, without our half dimension of time, is next to meaningless. Walking a long distance only takes a long time when you are bound by the passage of time! So, when Scriptures tell us God is omnipresent, everywhere in both time and space, they may simply be telling us that He and all of His host are outside of time as we know it. Does all this seem too speculative, too aerie-faerie, or unlikely and unscientific?

Well, according to the latest physics theories, there are at least six other dimensions to time. There had to be at least five more dimensions, say many theorists, for the "Big Bang" to work. In other words, outside our present existence, outside our three dimensions of space and half dimension of time—where God is—scientists now are certain time has more real dimensions than the one, or half one, that we live in. Only we, in our mortal lives, are presently hooked to the towrope. The Creator, as He attests, is not.

Are you starting to see the possibilities here? If the scientists are right, that there were (and are in His place) more dimensions to time than our own current one, then scientists have actually discovered a major reason why God can be the very logical and practical alternative to the "Big Bang" and evolution. Time, as we have always known it, and which many scientists have claimed denies the plausibility of the Creation account, is not the way it always has been, nor the way it need be for the One who created it. There is, therefore, even less truly objective or scientific reason not to believe in God. It's still simply a matter of choice. "Big bang," or God. Or some other god.

There is nothing illogical, unreasonable, or unscientific about God, just as the Bible describes Him. If there are more dimensions to time, somewhere out there, and He dwells out there beyond our space and our time, He is reasonably and logically eternal, never aging or wearying, never limited to before or after, never confined to any vicinity, anywhere in space. Without time, the meaning of distance as a limitation, as tiring the traveler, or taking a while, disappears. That's pretty much what Einstein theorized half a century ago, in the theory of relativity. And he was still, for the most part, just thinking about our half-dimension of time.

Obviously, our ideas and understanding of time are very pivotal in how we comprehend Genesis and the effectiveness of any apologetic (defense of the faith) we can muster from the Creation account. Our interpretations of Scripture are often greatly influenced by our understandings and assumptions about time. Most of us, for instance, know that both Peter, and the Psalmist before him, said something to the effect that a thousand years is as a day to the Lord. That has often been presented as a solid equation, like a quarter of a cup is four ounces. Is that right, however? Is it a literal fact, or is it more a literary or figurative phrasing, about the same as saying "people are like grasshoppers" (Isaiah and Exodus)? I think it's probably in the same category as "grasshoppers." In fact, the equation "1 day = 1,000 years" would seem to put a time and speed limit on God, letting Him be, at best, only "almost" independent of time and space.

Throughout history, our experience of time has definitely left us with pretty narrow, and perhaps naive, ideas about time. Consequently, I think we may have often misunderstood prophecies. For instance, God might say something to the effect of "I will destroy Jerusalem," or "the bones of so-and-so will be scattered." As far as He, whose word is or becomes reality, is concerned, such prophecies were a "done deal" as soon as He declared them.

But things appeared to us a bit differently. Men often assumed "tomorrow," when even centuries were to pass by before the reality of the prophecy came into our dimension. There was a great deal of confusion about Jesus' coming. And the prophecies of Daniel and the seventy weeks (or 490 years) add another rather interesting wrinkle to our confusion. They reveal that "God's time," or time reckoning, can even be "taken out of gear," or "put in neutral," so to speak, and later be put back "into gear," as far as we are concerned. At least that's what many Bible scholars think: The seventy weeks apparently started, stopped, and restarted; and many students of prophecy think they will restart again for the completion of the seven years of tribulation described in the Book of Revelation. That "slippage," that apparent disconnect between "our time" and "His time," could be a key to understanding how the Creator worked in the six "Creation-days" of Genesis.

So let's talk about the Creation account now. We've previously discussed how the Creation account separates Genesis 1:1 from the rest of the account. We also know the rest of the Creation has been divided into six portions, or six periods. The six periods, or segments, have traditionally been rendered "days." Most of us have assumed them to be twenty-four-hour days, probably picturing them as midnight to midnight, Monday through Saturday, and we've squeezed the full completion of all the events described into the confines of a 144-hour "work week." We need to look closely at the original language and scriptural organization and structure of Genesis 1 and 2 and compare them to other Scriptures and to some natural world events.

Other than the six "days" (as translated), Genesis 1 never gives any dates or measurements of time. Are those "days" a literal fact, or are they a literary idea as we discussed above, or are they simply an artifact (ungrounded result) of translation? What does the Bible actually say in regard to them, and how does it relate them one to another and the events of creation described?

In 1611, the King James translators chose to translate *yowm*, as "day." *Yowm* is a Hebrew word that has a much broader set of meanings. *Yowm* also translates as just a part of a twenty-four-hour equatorial day (always the daylight part). And *yowm* translates as a season, as a year, as an indefinite or definite period of time, and as an epoch or era. It's any period of time. Its appropriate meaning depends on the need and the context of the speaker. The period needn't even be exact. *Yowm* can simply designate a collection of days, hours, or years defined by something else, such as a season, a lifetime, a king's reign, or a period of labor, etc. Many times *yowm* simply points toward a specific event, as "in that day," or the "Day of the Lord." Maybe the "day of the dinosaur." A good example is in Genesis 2:17, where *yowm* only points to a certain beginning of something that will then take a long time to manifest ("... *in the day that thou eatest thereof thou shalt surely die*").

So, you see, the word *yowm*, does not necessarily specify a twenty-four-hour period. *Yowm* is far from being an easy one-to-one, it-always-means-this word. It allows for wide choice in translation. Choosing a meaning for *yowm* is not going to answer our questions. It cannot by itself tell us how much time God took to actually complete the Creation. We need other clues, other context, to truly inform us whether He took six days—144 hours, or six eons—any number of days, years, or centuries.

As we've said, the creation works of Genesis 1:1 were presumably finished before any of the factors were ready that would make a literal twenty-four-hour day, or a day-light day, possible (a solid earth, rotation, and sunlight, etc.). Since I've already made the case for setting verse 1, and the creating described in it, into a separate time-period outside the rest of Genesis 1 and 2, let's just leave it aside and not even have it a part of our "day" discussion. We can start with verses 2 through 5.

But the situation here is rather similar: The conditions that would provide "morning" and "evening," and the events that lead us to call twenty-four hours a "day," are not yet in place. The light necessary to cause the "morning" is only created in verses 3 and 4. It is sunlight shining upon the earth's surface that creates a traveling band of morning and evening that separate night and day. As we've already discussed, if God used the natural processes we see going on elsewhere in the universe, the sun was not turned on exactly like an electric light, but more likely a slowly sputtering oil lamp. And the clearing of space and atmosphere was probably a long process. So the "bracketing" morning and evening could not be there until 3 and 4 are accomplished, and then we also face a question of "where." Both morning and evening are traveling around the globe at about 1,000 mph! And it may well have been different then, as the earth is slowing down, and "days"—if equal to one rotation—might have been only minutes long, long ago. Like everything about time, things are relative.

These may be only technicalities and "picky points," but they are real issues, and often a problem to scientists, theologians, and our children. And they expose our inability to be completely sure, and why simple assumptions about interpreting a *yowm* can confuse and mislead us. God, we know, is not the author of confusion, nor is He intending to mislead us. Maybe our assumptions and translation are creating problems for us.

How about trying another later "day?" Try verse 13: *"And the evening and the morning were the third day."* Does that mean that all the preceding works of verses 9 through 12 were done in "day" three? Then all the waters over all the earth receded and gathered into seas, the land appeared and dried, some rock was made into sand, sand was made into soil; all the plants throughout the history of the earth were created, established, flourished, and perhaps some were extinct, all within day three. In twenty-four hours. That's a lot. What a rush of mighty waters that must have been! Think of the plate tectonics involved, moving all the mass and weight off of one plate or onto the edges of others, etc. Who knows, maybe that's why the earth tilted on its axis?

It's also interesting to note, that in contrast, in "day" one, only one actual event took place: Light appeared, and darkness versus light was defined. That could have taken a billion years, of course, or been done in a mere "click" of time! Time is so relative. Certainly to us, and most likely, to our Creator!

Maybe we should look again at the "day." If we do look closely, we can notice several facts. First, nothing says the creations of verses 9 through 12 were done all within the *yowm*. The works of that "day" were described and ordered. Then we are told that they came to be exactly according to plan. Then we read that God inspected the results and was satisfied that they were either done, or being done, well—as He so intended. If God is working in our time, as the translators probably assumed, everything would have had to be done in that time frame, right? Well, not exactly. Everyone, every believer, I think, can agree that He could have "seen" it finished in the future. Or He could have simply known the outcome of His will would be absolutely what He willed. But if He is not confined to our dimension of time, well, then it's a whole new ball game. Nothing had to be done instantly, or magically. And nothing in the scriptural account has to radically contradict what science believes.

You see, the modern science outline of events essentially agrees with that land-sea scenario in verses 6 through 9, and the appearances of plant life in verses 11 and 12 (sans evolution), but definitely not in eight, or even twenty-four hours. Time, you see, is the toughest issue for us to deal with in defending or promoting Genesis as the true Creation history. Evolution, as the creative mechanism of our planet, may be a dearly-held belief in science, but it's still, in all honesty, only a competing theory, which must best fit the facts and data to win the competition—and it is not doing so well, as the facts and data continue to accumulate. But the evidences and apparent "facts" about time pose very serious problems for the credibility, or theoretical effectiveness, of the Creation account. The big problem stems from interpreting *yowm* as a twenty-four-hour day. It only gets bigger when we insist the six days are contiguous, that they are fully compressed into a 144-hour week, and there is no time elapsing between them. That is saying that all the history of the earth, up to and including Adam, is 144 hours long, our time.

Suppose we choose not to define *yowm* as a twenty-four-hour day and do not make the assumption that the "day" is even necessarily the total or actual time of the creating works of any group of verses preceding, and bracketed by, these numbered *yowm*. What do we come up with? Maybe we simply have just six or seven designated periods, or "sets," of Creation. If God does create by merely speaking it, or by issuing the command that things be made or become as He wishes, maybe we have six announcements and a concluding "and the thing was done." It's certainly consistent with *yowm* as an epoch or era, or as even a short period of time followed by a long one. It's consistent with something begun or set into motion, but not immediately accomplished or even yet finished—such as His seventh day of rest! Think about it.

If we were creating and planting gardens or vineyards, we would say, "And the third one was done." Yet all we really have is some little rooted sticks in the ground; we merely know (within human limitations) that vineyard number three will eventually be a done deal. All we need to do, we trust, is let nature (God's perfect natural laws?) and our field hands (God's perfect Son?) finish the work. Suppose you were the owner of Microsoft. In a meeting with all the officers and department heads, you outlined a new product and assigned the work. Though you set only an approximate finish date, you would still expect your plans and directives to be as good as accomplished. You could confidently announce, "Windows 98 is on its way, and it will be a revolutionary product." How much more confident and able is God? Could the *yowm* not be something similar, a time of planning, assignment, and announcement of the new set of creations?

But what about those "evenings" and "mornings" that are announced with each *yowm* of Creation. There are a few things we should consider about them as well. If the "mornings" and "evenings" really are mornings and evenings, they are backward. They actually bracket the dark, and not any of the daylight part of the twenty-four-hour cycle which *yowm* would normally represent in the Hebrew language. Some authorities that know Jewish historical customs have defended that reverse order by pointing out it is a traditional custom of the Jews to reckon a day/evening to morning. That's true, but you have a chicken-and-egg problem here. Most scholars are convinced the Jews reckoned a day that way, reversing the world norm, simply because of their interpretation of Genesis 1.

Some of you may reasonably ask, "Shouldn't we accept the Jewish interpretation of Genesis as correct?" If the Jews, even up to the time of Jesus, had had continuous possession of the written texts and maintained fluency in their old tongue, I might answer "yes" without reservations. However, the Jews had long periods in their history when the text was missing, lost and unread, even forgotten. At the same time, the language they were using was changing and drifting into new spoken and written forms. When they did recover a written text, they had much the same problems we have: deciphering and interpreting a complex old-fashioned script without vowels and punctuation and employing a half-forgotten vocabulary.

That leads us to another very interesting possibility. It requires questioning some tradition and assumptions again. I don't wish to insist it's correct, but it's definitely an interesting possibility. The word "evening" is translated from *ereb*. *Ereb* is considered by scholars to be derived from *arab*. *Arab* is, essentially, a "twin" when written. Do you remember that the written Hebrew had no vowels? So *ereb* and *arab* are identical in the ancient Hebrew written language. The reader must choose between them. So must the translator. *Ereb*, translates as "dusk," or "evening." *Arab*, translates as "pledge," "guarantee," or as "given as a pledge," or "a surety, a sure thing." Now, the opening verb of each of the six verses that refer to the *yowm*, is *hayah*, our familiar "let there be" or "let it be so." So we could translate the combination of those two words as something like "It was so pledged in surety" or "It was sure to be so." What a way to end a Creation—*yowm!*

What about the "morning"? "Morning" is translated from *boqer*. Well, we have the same situation as with *ereb!* *Boqer* is also believed to be derived from a "twin," *baqar*. *Baqar* translates as "to plow" (a creative act), or even more importantly, "to break forth"! Now put those two together. Verses 5, 8, 13, and so on, could be interpreted as referring to the preceding *yowm* of creations and be saying: "It is pledged (God's pledge) and guaranteed to be so and will come forth that way," instead of that curious *"and the evening and morning were the first (or second, or third, etc.) day."* In other words, it could be saying that God assured and pledged the things He ordered would indeed become exactly so after each *yowm*.

How plausible is this new interpretation of the original? How much credibility should we accord it? Of course, each of us must decide on every change proposed here, but I think several factors weight heavily in favor of the new interpretation. Three words are involved. If *yowm* is assumed to refer to a twenty-four-hour day, then *ereb* and *boqer*, translated as "evening" and "morning," are perhaps most logical, though the phrasing is awkward, if not contradictory. The meaning is a bit unclear, and the traditional version contradicts modern scientific evidence and logic in a big way. If *yowm* need not refer to a twenty-four-hour day, or we do not insist that the "creative sessions" (even if they were twenty-four-hour days) were absolutely sequential and running end-to-end in a 144-hour stretch, then "evening" and "morning" are much less likely or sensible. And *arab* and *baqar* are good choices, make sensible translations, and can fit very well in several interpretations that do not contradict modern science. And the new interpretation fits very well with our understanding of God and His abilities and ways.

There's another Scripture I believe supports the feasibility of this new interpretation. I've mentioned it before. John 1:1-3 tells us that Jesus created everything: *"All things were made by him; and without him was not any thing made that was made."* That certainly sounds like our Microsoft scenario. I think we can reasonably envision God as the president, or commander in chief, and Jesus as his CEO. If that be true, there is certainly no reason that God would doubt His idea, or Word, would ever be anything less than perfectly completed (or *hayah*), from the moment He first proclaimed even a billion-year development process. I am sure He could, in keeping with the new interpretation, conclude each *yowm's* pronouncements with the pledge and guarantee that it shall be exactly so.

We might also conclude from what we see and read of our natural world, God rarely uses instantaneous miracles, but usually allows natural events to manifest His will, His purposes, and His prophecies. Real kings, and natural events, such as weather and earthquakes, are often His agents. Miracles, I believe, are almost always for display of His might and glory, to help us trust and believe in Him. Before Adam, who was supposed to be impressed by anything miraculous? Surely, He didn't need to use miraculous, instantaneous processes because He was short of time! He could easily wait out the waters receding, land drying, and so on. I believe God is always a God of law and of order, and I believe it is consistent that He allowed eons of His own natural laws and processes, working in the earth in the earth's time to accomplish such results. The only thing that militates against this is the six 24-hour "days" translation.

As we move ahead in the Creation account and continue looking carefully at the "create" verbs used in the Hebrew, there will be uncovered even more support for the commanded-it-be-done understanding. So continue, if you're not yet persuaded, to at least suspend any hard-line conclusions about time and time scales, the "days," and the six "days," interpretations.

Before we conclude this chapter, I want to look a little bit more at Creation-day four.

> Genesis 1:16 *And God made two great lights; the greater light to rule the day, and the lesser light to rule the night: he made the stars also.*
> Genesis 1:17 *And God set them in the firmament of the heaven to give light upon the earth.*
> Genesis 1:18 *And to rule over the day and over the night, and to divide the light from the darkness: and . . ."*

This seems to be going over old ground. Though the moon has not been mentioned before, at best, this passage seems to be using up three verses in an otherwise very economical Creation account, all for very little advancement of the story. It certainly seemed, in earlier verses, that the sun was already made and its nuclear fire lighted. We've also already had an accounting for the stars. So what's the point here? I don't want to take the time to go through the original three verses word by word here, but I think we might do the original more justice, and promote our understanding, if we paraphrased them like this:

> Genesis 1:16 "Now, God made the two great lights; the greater [the sun] to rule the day, and the lesser [the moon] to rule the night, even the stars." [The "he made" in the *"he made the stars"* was not in the original, but was added by the translators.]
> Genesis 1:17 "He set them in the heavens above the clouds to shine with glory upon the earth"
> Genesis 1:18 "and to have the power over day and night, and make the difference between the cheer of light and utter darkness. And . . ."

I think we accomplish a couple of things in this interpretation. I think it shows the KJV language ignored some subtle shifting of the sense of the Hebrew, regarding light and darkness and shine and rule, and so forth. That is why verses 16 through 18 seem so repetitive of earlier information. Our paraphrase suggests the verses

Let the Earth Bring Forth ... Life

are intended to tell us about design and purpose in this part of God's creation as it relates to mankind. And in this way, in this paraphrase, the verses are not exceptionally repetitive.

This, by the way, is the first time the moon is mentioned. Is that significant? It might well be. As we've seen before, position in the Creation outline can be important information itself. So what about the moon?

Well, scientists generally believe that the moon is quite a bit younger than the earth. If Creation-day four does indicate that the moon just now appeared in this creation period, then it is confirming that belief that the moon is younger than the earth. But scientists are also a little perplexed by the moon. The moon is actually much too big for this planet. It doesn't quite fit in with normal physical and astronomical rules. If it really is younger, that means it did indeed come "swooping in" well after Earth was developed. By all rights (or natural laws), it should have crashed into us, pulled us apart, or disrupted our stable orbit, depending on exactly how it came into our proximity. Why? Because it's so big and so close that its powerful gravity, even now, continually deforms the earth and swishes the seas back and forth in their tidal flows and wobbles us in our orbit—it's still right on the verge of being a real troublemaker. Yet there it is, hanging out there in such a perfect balance—in just the right orbit, and so on—that it's almost a miracle that it got there so perfectly and that it all works, actually helping our ecology and improving our quality of life.

If it is all by God's design, who's to be surprised? But if is merely by accident, a runaway little planet that just luckily slipped into such an improbable orbit well, that just gives scientists another little mystery they have to overlook or keep working on to explain, by exceptional theories about exceptional events and situations!

Sometimes, I think, that God is just too easy an answer for scientists! I also suspect this moon thing is another signpost of sorts that they just don't want to see.

CHAPTER FOUR

WHAT ABOUT DINOSAURS?

I have a collection of rocks, about a dozen gray-tan pieces, some what the size and shape of pies. They came from the top of one of the highest peaks in the Oregon Cascades. They're a mudstone that scientists say originated on the floor of a cold wet forest about 210 million years ago. They're fairly soft and layered tightly like pages in a book. If you grasp them firmly and pull the "pages" apart, they open up to reveal layers of perfectly preserved leaves from the trees of the ancient forest. The leaves look like they dropped yesterday. I can't personally vouch for their age, but I can attest to their having come from a tiny up-thrust peak in Oregon, where no muddy forest floors could accumulate now. I'd say they are a pretty convincing evidence of plate tectonics in action, and some would say they are equally convincing proof that life on earth has a very long history.

One of the more interesting things about these fossils, and the bit of forest preserved on that mountaintop, is that no remains or evidence of animal or insect life has ever been found. Not even signs of chewing on the leaves. It's curiously disappointing.

I think that most of us, when we think of life, think of animals, not plants. We'd much rather go to a zoo than an arboretum, watch a documentary about bears or lions rather than ferns, and have fossils of "creatures" rather than of trees. For those of you who share such preferences, this is your day coming up—Creation-day five. The record of the plants is done, and from here on it's all about animals.

You might wonder whether, because the creation of plants was entirely accounted for in Creation-day four and animals begin in Creation-day five, that means all the plants were created first, before any animals. Would that explain my fossil collection? I don't think so. For one thing, there are many other fossil deposits that don't tell the same tale. In fact, as far as the fossil record is concerned, throughout the world it generally appears that both plants and animals appear together almost from the beginning. In fact, once life got rolling, both animals and plants were here together, and it looks very much like they both moved along more or less in a parallel sequence, from simpler to more complex, from lower to higher levels. The evidence is strong that both plants and animals showed up mutually integrated into whole and balanced ecological systems from very early times. There were plants and plant eaters (and plant-eater eaters) well knit together at every stage. God's design and execution of the Creation was always balanced and complete.

Paleontology and geology are continuing to show, from the evidences they obtain from the natural world, that the creations initiated in Creation-day five were manifesting along with those initiated in Creation-day four, not separately and afterwards. That, too, strongly suggests that the *yowm* were not merely consecutive twenty-four hour days, nor even separate consecutive periods of time, of completed creation. The plants accounted for, and purposed in Creation-day four, were more likely the subject of that "day's" work of the Creator. The work wasn't finished, but initiated and programmed for development. On Creation-day five, animals were the subject. The first of them were created about the same time as the first plants (animals generally need plants already present and on the dinner table). The idea here is similar to the idea that the president of Microsoft meets on Monday to get staff working on his plans for business software and meets on Tuesday to get staff also working on personal computer software.

If we were to continue our scenario of the last chapter, where you were putting together an estate, a small "garden of Eden," for the new corporate CEO, you might have had the basic landscaping in before you started bringing in any of the fish and animals; but you still had more plants on order and were still shopping for canaries and horses. There's a lot of evidence that our world was designed and developed in a similar fashion. By the way, when you imagined yourself creating the estate, did your plan include flies, fleas, and mosquitoes? I know they make good feed for fish, frogs, and birds, but really. . . .

As we pick up the narrative of the Genesis account putting together its Garden of Eden we read:

> Genesis 1:20 *And God said, Let the waters bring forth abundantly the moving creature that hath life, and fowl that may fly above the earth in the open firmament of heaven.*

We don't have look too closely to spot some familiar language. Verse 20 sounds a lot like verse 11, except it's the waters that are to bring forth. And that in itself, is pretty interesting. *"Let the waters bring forth . . . the moving creature"* is practically a journalistic scoop on the scientific tabloids: "Proof Is Found: Animal Life Originated In Water!" Remember our earlier discussion about scientists trying to generate life out of muck and now turning their attention to certain sterile clays? Well, part of that shift comes from the fact that modern theory is quite unanimous now; life actually originated in some shallow backwaters (not the gathered sea). So this bit of Genesis beats out the headlines of "Science News" by about 3500 years. I guess we could call that another signpost. Furthermore, it's not just a sensational headline; it comes with a pretty good story as well. We just need to put on our translator's hat and start ferreting out the rest of the story.

Let's tackle the whole first phrase at once, *"Let the waters bring forth abundantly the moving creature that hath life,"* but start with just *"the waters."* "The waters" is translated from *mayim*, the same word we had in Genesis 1:2. In that verse, *mayim*, which means "shallows" or "swamps," and useless "waste waters," was used to draw our attention to the fact that all the waters of the earth were spread out as a shallow lake, and God intended to gather them together to form both a sea and dry land. Here again the word is used to point out that we are still to focus on "shallows," only now they are the remnants, shallow lakes and ponds, and either sterile (if plant life—algae, etc.—is not yet established) or swampy marshes, developing with the early plants, which early animals may need to feed upon.

So Genesis tells us explicitly here, the *mayim* are to be the first place, the environment of origins, the seat of creation, for the first animal life. "Let the *mayim* bring forth abundantly the moving creature that hath life." As we look more into the Hebrew language, an even more vibrant picture is painted there; something you've only seen if you've had the opportunity to look at a drop of pond water under a microscope!

WHAT ABOUT DINOSAURS?

We need to look at the Hebrew words translated as the "critters" here, the *"moving creatures that hath life."* There are several words combined actually, used to build up the picture of our swamp-water zoo. The first, of importance, is *sharats*. It's translated, *"Let . . . bring forth abundantly."* That's a bit misleading. It sounds too much like we have another create-verb in the Hebrew (like *bara* or *hayah*), when we do not. *Sharats* would be better translated as "Let . . . teem," or "Let . . . swarm forth" these living things! The phrase says, "Let the waters swarm and teem with [the critters]. . . ." That's vivid enough I think, but it only gets better!

The critters (or "the moving creatures") is a translation of two words in the Hebrew. First is *sherets*, which emphatically augments and continues the meanings and implications of *sharats*. *Sherets* means "moving things that swarm and teem." It connotes critters that creep and scurry, swirl and dance, and swarm and skitter, in massive numbers. It is especially used of insects, the tiniest reptiles, and quadrupeds. One dictionary defines *sherets* as: "an active mass of minute animals." The second word underlying the translation moving creature, is *nephesh*, which particularly refers to "breathing life" (hence, animal, not plant), the animalistic qualities of appetites and will, and the characteristic activity and mobility of animals. Genesis intends that we have no doubt of what sort of life is to begin teeming in the marshy waters. It is animals that have appetites, and have the will and ability to "go get it" to satisfy them. We are not the only ones with appetites and wills, even the smallest and even the first have them!

These three words together, *sharats, sherets,* and *nephesh*, describe the creatures themselves. They are as much adjectives as nouns; colors as substance. But one more word is used, lest we have any doubt what is being created here, a word which the King James Version translates *"that hath life."* The original Hebrew is *chay* (pronounced ka-ee). *Chay* is another word that emphasizes the liveliness, the animation, the very essence of the "living-ness" of animal creatures. It also carries the sense of the "community-ness" of such creatures, signifies even such ideas as a "congregation," and (I like this one) "the merry multitude of running, springing troops of things"! That last comes out of Strong's dictionary, the source for biblical translating. In short, that which "hath life," hath vitality—and it hath *chay!*

Can there be any doubt about what God was describing? Can't you just see a pond, full of wriggling, swimming, scooting things like bugs, tadpoles, and—whatever? It didn't even take that much work to bring it out, to elaborate, and to flesh out with the fuller detail of the Hebrew. The next part of the verse, however, is more seriously flawed in the King James translation.

The second part of Genesis 1:20 reads: ". . . *and fowl that may fly above the earth . . .*" A casual reader, or one unconcerned with Genesis as a scientifically useful text, will miss the problem. It looks to be a rather straightforward and logical advancement of the Creation thesis. As expected, it appears to describe an entirely new, second set of animal life-types. Yet critics of the Genesis account often cite this verse as another glaring example of error by the writer. And just what's the problem?

"Birds," they will advise scornfully, "come late in the fossil record. Birds are hardly one of the lower, earlier life forms. If Genesis really is supposed to be an actual record of the appearance of life on earth, and even if we are willing to ignore the matter about those 'six days,' well, you still have a real problem! The birds are absolutely out of place. There is no doubt that birds don't even appear until after the dinosaurs. Face it, the Bible misses again!"

Well, let's deflate their argument a little. No, let's totally deflate it!

I hope you've started realizing by now that the ancient Hebrews thought differently, saw the world differently, and described it differently than we do today. The features they thought were the important ones to use to categorize and describe things and to build words around—the classificatory principles of their language and perception—were quite different from ours. That is to say, the features and qualities that would qualify individual things to be in a group, which they would name in one word, are quite different from ours. And the features they would use to describe an individual, or a group, are quite different from ours.

Every society and its language works that way. Every society has a different way of seeing and evaluating the world around them and creates a language that has a different way of sorting, classifying, and naming things they see in the world. That's one reason it is so difficult to learn a second language, especially as you get older and more set in the ways you categorize and describe things. That's one reason it's not so hard to read something written in your second language, but its much more difficult to speak—"invent into"— the second language

To us, the word "bird" may include everything from hummingbird to sparrow, to crow, to eagle, to ostrich. But the ostrich would not probably be included with other birds in a single word or intended when the "bird" word was used by the ancient Hebrews. Hummingbirds, for that matter, might also be in a different category from most birds. Why? Because the Hebrews tended to notice more how things moved than by their shapes or anatomical classifications. Ostriches don't fly. Hummingbirds fly, but so differently from other birds that they might have been grouped in a whole different word from sparrows and hawks. I don't know for sure, but it's a good guess. In the same way, following the same principle, an ancient Hebrew would probably have had one word that stood for scooters, tricycles, wagons, and automobiles. They all roll on wheels.

There is good reason, of course, for our having taken this little "rabbit trail" into how the ancient Hebrews thought, and how the way they viewed the world affected their linguistics and choice of words. It should help us understand a number of details in the Creation account, especially as we deal with animal life.

For instance, consider the word *owph*. It is *owph* that is translated "fowl" in the King James's rendition of verse 20; *"and fowl that may fly above the earth,"* and as "birds" in the New International Version and other versions. It is translating *owph* as "birds" in this place in the Creation account that raises the conflict with science, and a rather well-documented fossil record. And, I think, translating *owph* as "birds" in this particular verse is an example of not really understanding the Hebrew mind and linguistic categories and letting our expectations and assumptions take the lead in guiding our translating. The fact is the word could refer to birds. And then, again, it might not. In many contexts throughout the Bible, where there is no doubt the speaker means "bird," *owph* does stand alone as a word for indicating birds. That may be that is why it has commonly interpreted as "something covered with feathers that flies"—birds. But from its roots, *owph,* in and of itself, more likely means only "something that flies," or "something covered with wings." "Feathers" were not a part of it.

That "something that flies" picks up the essential aspect of motion the Hebrews were most concerned with and doesn't commit us to any further conclusions which might lead us astray. We need to rely, as we must so often in the Hebrew, on the context and what else is said in the Scripture. The King James Version, and most interpreters, simply assumed that these *owph* are birds. The feathers were thrown in for free. After all, what else flies? Well, how about bugs? A great many insects fly. Were they considered at all in 1611? We don't know, of course. Maybe insects were just a bit too lowly, a little below the line of sight of the translators, to occur to them. It might be a similar situation to that which appears to have happened earlier in the translation involving the algae.

There's more at stake here in this choice between birds and insects than just reconciling our text with the latest beliefs in science. It's equally a matter of accuracy and knowing the truth of the Genesis account. As for the science, here's the situation. As best science can tell insects really were the first animal life to venture on to dry ground. The prevailing theory, in fact, has it that insects originated in such watery environs as Genesis describes; they became the first creatures to venture out into the land; and those that led the way furthest abroad and even dominated the land for eons, were winged, "flying creatures." So, if *owph* refers to insects and not birds here, Genesis is still moving right along, matching step-by-step the scientific outline of origins. The contradiction, "birds out of place," disappears and is replaced instead by another "win" in the paradigm and prediction game.

Is this letting science lead or dictate our translating, here? No not at all. Not leading, just helping. We are letting science give us important clues as to how to best interpret this terse account written in this once lost and forgotten language. These clues can help us rediscover some details and accuracy that was of no import for a couple of millennia. As we try to choose our interpretation of *owph*, authorities can, as I've said, be found for either interpretation, insect or bird. Science surely can offer several reasons to choose "insect," but if I had only the scientific backing for a choice, I would really hesitate to overturn the traditional. But there's some equally convincing linguistic and scriptural evidence on the side of insects as well!

Here are some facts about the linguistic evidence in verse 20. Let's just assume that these first *owph* are insects, that most of them had wings (many, like beetles, are literally "covered with wings"), and most could fly, thus meeting with the translation *"that may fly above the earth."* Even that is giving away more than we need, because as far as I can see, it could just as easily be translated as, "*owph* may flee the waters and spread out across through the land and the sky," but we don't really even need to get into that to make a good argument that the *owph*, here, are insects. We have plenty enough other supporting evidence.

For instance, notice that the verse did not separate the *owph* from the *sherets*. It said "Let the waters teem and bring forth the *sherets,* and the *owph."* That would not be consistent, or logical, if the *owph* were birds, right? I think it's clear both are coming forth from the waters, and amongst them are insects that may (not will, or must) fly across or above the land. Now, a second point: *Sherets,* which is so closely associated with the *owph* here, always refers to minute and tiny things, insects in particular, and never to birds. And a third point: The *sharats,* which is what gave us our *"Let [the waters] bring forth"* in the King James, and which we understand really says "teem" or "swarm" (it also translates "wriggle"), applies to the *owph,* as well. Teem, swarm, and wriggle all sound much more like insects than birds, to me.

To recap verse 20: What we've seen is that God first created a profusion of *sherets,* all simpler and smaller living creatures in the shallows and swamps of this lavish garden He was cultivating on the earth. The three words the Scripture uses, *sharats, sherets,* and *nephesh,* all combine to paint a picture that reasonably includes swarming, teeming little things, bacteria, protozoa, insects, perhaps even small amphibians, reptiles, and other small animals. These teeming, swarming little hordes of creatures start in the *mayim* of (probably) tropical swamps and marshes but (soon?) include among them some that can leave the water and fly into the sky and "swarm and teem" over the land as well.

Now there's more to verse 20 than what we've covered so far, but we're going to have to come back to it after we finish with verse 21. By then, we will have both discovered more evidence to support our choice of insects, and some very interesting implications about both the *sherets* and *owph.*

The next verse, Genesis 1:21, may cover less time in the overall scientific perspective and the equivalent part of the fossil record, but it's a really big one for most of us. Among other things, verse 21 opens the gate into Jurassic Park! Verse 21 gives us the dinosaurs!

> Genesis 1:21 *And God created great whales, and every living creature that moveth, which the waters brought forth abundantly, after their kind, and every winged fowl after his kind . . .*

One brief phrase—five words in the King James Version—tells us about events that modern scientists think took place over a couple hundred million years. A truly modern, "Family-Friendly Living Translation Bible" (this is imaginary, of course), might well retranslate *"And God created great whales,"* as "And God created the real Jurassic Park." Why? Well, if you haven't already guessed, "whales" should have been "dinosaurs." Before we get into the details, let's go over some background.

If you look at a science textbook, you'll find that in the scientists' outline and in their fossil record and geologic time chart, the events of verse 21 are placed in a time period called the "Mesozoic Era." They named it that because they used to think that those years, from about 225 million to 65 million years ago, encompassed the middle of the earth's natural (life) history. Mesozoic means "middle life."

The first dinosaurs, we are told, had begun to walk the earth a bit earlier, say at about 250 million years ago. The Jurassic, which most of us know from a famous movie about dinosaurs, was the period of their greatest dominion, but they remained earth's greatest creatures right up to the end of their time when they suddenly all disappeared. At least, so it appears in the fossil record. Science also tells us that late in the era, toward the end of it (though the latest theories keep revising the estimates to less late), birds "appeared" in the fossil-record, as well as the earliest mammals. Without any reference to a time scale, the outline of Genesis's Creation account completely agrees!

I've put a chart (Chart A) in the back of this book for you to look at. It summarizes the scientific outline and pairs it with Genesis 1. As you can see there is a lot of agreement between them. The essential difference between the two outlines is, as we've continually pointed out, in the scientists' attachment of absolute dates and a time scale to their outline. Of course, by now we shouldn't really care. If we ourselves are not locked into a time scale, the scriptural record not only holds its own but, as I see it, rather outdoes the scientific outline by having published it first. We can happily respond, "So, what else is new?"

While you're looking at that chart, you might also look at Chart B. That one shows just how much of the evolutionary story is not even good theory but pure imagination, fabrication, or Evolutionist faith. The chart is adapted from a recent book aimed at children and the general public. The book, very typically, presents evolution as a simple fact, "the way nature works." You'll see how this, in the original version, purports to show how much evidence has been compiled to substantiate and complete the evolutionary story of mammals. At first glance (which is all anyone is expected to give), it was pretty convincing. It looked like the fossil record is indeed full and strong, almost complete. All one has to do is "connect the dots" (the fossil shapes that make up the fossil record)—and they would have us believe that's what they did—to see that the "dots" are so many and so well-placed that they form a complete picture, and all the various the evolutionary histories of the illustration are proven.

The readers are supposed to be convinced that all the necessary evolutionary linkages (or "missing links") have been found, proving the evolutionary histories of the mammal species. We're supposed to go away believing the Evolutionary story that evolution is proven, no longer even a theory. It took a computer-aided color analysis to show that there is not one evolutionary relationship (one biological descent history) shown there that is known or proven. The casual reader of that book would never have known that. Why? Not because of any direct untruth, but because the truth was very effectively obscured by a very deceptive design. Check it out, you'll see exactly what I mean—and why the Genesis Creation theory should be at least as convincing!

Let's get to work on Genesis 1:21. You'll see here just how well the sequence, that is, the order of appearances of dinosaurs, mammals, and birds, matches the scientific outline.

The first act, or set of creations, in the verse is *"And God created great whales."* The ancient Hebrews had a word, *tanniyn,* which we would pronounce "tan-neen," that practically expressed terror. As usual, it referred to, or included, a group of possible or actual types of creatures. *Tanniyn* could be referring to dragons, land monsters, sea monsters, or sea serpents. Only this once, in all the Scripture, has it been thought to be a whale. As a member of the collective referents of the Hebrew word, whale is something of a misfit. The root word from which *tanniyn* derives, we are told by the authoritative Strong's dictionary, refers to a monster or hideous land animal, and another popular dictionary actually suggests it could refer to an extinct dinosaur.

Should we have much doubt at all that this first part of verse 21 should probably read, "And God created the great dinosaurs"? Even more, the Hebrew word being translated "great," here, is *gadowl.* Now, *gadowl* really meant great. Look at this list of additional meanings, or qualities, for *gadowl* and think about them being paired with *tanniyn:* "insolent, loud, intense, mighty, noble, exceedingly haughty and proud, high, long"! So you tell me, did

"HEY MOM, WHAT ABOUT DINOSAURS?"

God impress His scribe (Moses?) with a proper image of dinosaurs, or not? Do you think these adjectives fit dinosaurs far better than whales? I've been privileged to boat alongside pods of whales in the Pacific, and they are indeed impressive. But I know meeting a single brontosaurus or tyrannosaurus would impress me a lot more, and I am sure I would be using just such *gadowl tanniyn* words in my description of my encounter!

Oh, to be sure, not all dinosaurs were huge, noble, or especially great. Scientists believe the first ones created were quite small (or so the fossils indicate) and the "bigness" and greatness came to be added as time passed and more were created (most scientists, of course, would say "evolved"). I have no reason to argue with the possibility that the first ones were small. It's very possible that God went from little critters in general in verse 20, to little dinosaurs in verse 21, and then to bigger ones, and bigger ones, and bigger ones, all the way up to the great big ones. I can almost imagine God starting out with the little ones first and saying, "Hey, I like these guys. How about some bigger ones?" And then saying, "Now those are pretty cool. How about some really big ones?" And looking at them, the real kings of the lizard kingdom, I can hear Him exclaiming, "Awesome!"

Why not? God could have had fun with Creation!

You might want to ask why the King James committee chose to translate *tanniyn* as "whale" instead of the other possibilities. I doubt we can answer that. It probably was a matter of their particular cultural needs and the "political correctness" of 1611. They certainly could have chosen "dragon." I think everyone knew what a dragon was, and many people believed that dragons existed. Perhaps "dragon" was rejected, however, because they felt dragons were more pagan or satanic and not of God. In fact, the "dragon" does represent Satan symbolically in numerous Scriptures, such as in Revelation. Similar reasoning may have led to rejecting all the

WHAT ABOUT DINOSAURS?

various monsters *tanniyn* could represent. But as for "dinosaurs," that particular word had not yet even been invented, and no one yet knew anything about them. No one except the ancient Hebrews scribes, it might seem.

Dinosaurs appear to be mentioned, and even described, in numerous Scriptures. The book of Job, considered the oldest book in the Bible, and perhaps an even older chapter of Jewish history, describes two specific *tanniyn*. "Behemoth" is described in Job 40:15-25, and "Leviathin," in Job 41:1–34. If you read those passages, you find the descriptions of each creature is a very close match with two identified species of dinosaur, but resemble nothing alive today. Some people, especially those who identify with that field of scholarship called "creation science" or "scientific creationism," think that Job thus shows men and dinosaurs walked the earth at the same time. They tend to argue for that because it would add support to their belief in the Creation-days being literal twenty-four-hour says, the six days being carried out in 144 hours, and the whole age of the earth (or universe) being about 6000 years. As you know, I do not agree. But I do believe that the creatures in Job are real dinosaurs. I believe also, however, that their descriptions were given to the author of Job by inspiration, and were not eyewitness accounts.

Let's get back to the Genesis account. Here is verse 21 again:

> Genesis 1:21 *And God created great whales, and every living creature that moveth, which the waters brought forth abundantly, after their kind, and every winged fowl after his kind and God saw that it was good.*

Let's second-guess that printer who, in 1550 A.D., divided the Scriptures into verses. Let's treat "And God created great dinosaurs" as a separate verse! It's certainly a significant enough event all by itself, I think, to warrant a separate verse. And there are a couple of other very good reasons that will become apparent as we go on. So let's temporarily call it "verse 21a."

One of the most intriguing things about this verse 21a is the create-verb used to "create" these dinosaurs. For only the second time in the Creation account, *bara* is used! *Bara*, remember, is that very personal, absolute, from scratch (some even say *ex nihilo*) creating-verb. It is used only three times in all the Creation account: First, referring to the creation of heaven and earth (the universe); second, in the creating of the dinosaurs; and third, it will be used when creating man, or Adam. This restricted usage remains remarkably consistent throughout the Scriptures. *Bara* is used in Genesis 6:7, when God laments He even *bara* man, and then brings the flood. It is used in Exodus 34:10, when God makes a covenant with the people Moses led and promised marvels (miracles) never before *bara*, never before done! It was used in Numbers 16:30, when God *bara* a "new thing" that consumed those who rebelled against Moses. It is used again in Deuteronomy 4:32, a Scripture recalling that God *bara* man. *Bara*, I think, is obviously, at the very least, a very special kind of "made." That it is used on this occasion, the creation of the dinosaurs, must catch our attention.

Surely, *bara* puts dinosaurs in a rather special category, giving them a quite unique standing in the Creation account. Could that have anything to do with that unique emotional chord that dinosaurs seem to strike in us? Why, after so long an absence from the earth, do they still loom large in every aspect of our modern culture—science, fiction, even in our children's interests and imaginations and toys (and how have they become such a big, unavoidable "in your face" challenge to our trust in the veracity of the Creation account?) As if these questions weren't enough, dinosaurs will only become even more of an enigma as we go on.

WHAT ABOUT DINOSAURS?

After "And God created the dinosaurs," we have our new verse:

Genesis 1:21b . . . *and every living creature that moveth, which the waters brought forth abundantly, after their kind, and every winged fowl after his kind and God saw that it was good.*

This sounds much like a repeat of verse 20. But it is not. There's actually a lot more information with some very significant details added here. And, we will now find our birds.

We can start with *"and every living creature that moveth, which the waters brought forth abundantly."* The first thing we need to take notice of is that *sharats* is used again here, with the same essential meaning as it had in verse 20, only the tense has been changed, and it now translates *"[the waters] brought forth abundantly."* So 21*b* can stand alone, not relying on 21*a* and its create-verb, *bara*. It doesn't look like these "living creature that moveth" are *bara*. And what are they? The "living creature," here, is translated from *chay*, and the waters are still the swampy *mayim*. But to properly understand the information of this sentence, we need to do some grammatical reconstruction and look at some new Hebrew vocabulary—some words that were pretty much lost, or obscured, in the King James translation.

Let's start by removing that comma between "moveth" and "which." It's not good grammar, but, like working out the solution to a Rubic cube puzzle, it's a useful step on the way to our reconstruction of the verse. Besides, remember, there is no punctuation in the original text; it's all been added by translators hoping to make things easier to read and understand. Sometimes it doesn't.

Now, as we do all this reconstructing and reinterpreting, keep in mind that this section of the Creation account (this time in Creation-day five) is completely about animals that originated and lived in the marshes and shallow waters. We just finished with the

"Hey Mom, What About Dinosaurs?"

great dinosaurs! So when we look at the next "every living creature," which is a perfectly good rendering of *chay*, we should not overlook the more precise, and very contrasting, meaning of the Hebrew word the King James Version (quite casually) translated as "that moveth." That's where we lost the track and the scientific precision of the message. After having just talked about dinosaurs, a simple "that moveth" doesn't tell the story. Not as it was to be heard by a Hebrew who was always so keenly interested in how "that creature moveth."

The Hebrew word behind "that moveth" is *ramas*. In this case, *ramas* refers to several kinds of movement, but not all kinds. When it refers to land animals, it means "to walk about on all fours," but "lightly," and not "heavily," in "short steps"—so this kind of "moveth" is, in all likelihood, not about the dinosaurs. This is the type of motion it signifies when applied to animals moving about on dry ground. But any of theses animals in verse 21*b* that might be walking on dry ground are still animals that either were originally created (as, say, a species), began their lives, or continue some part of their lives, in the watery environment! If *ramas* is being applied to animals still in the water environment, then *ramas* characterizes more of a move lightly, or "glide." Doesn't that remind you of a beaver or an amphibian like a salamander? So the insight available here is that these animals may be in both the dry and wet environment (amphibians!) and are definitely and deliberately being pictured in strong contrast with the dinosaurs of 21*a*. This phrase thus reads, essentially, "and all the many littler, or lesser animals that came from the waters."

Here's some scientific implications of the contrast we've drawn with our own translations. Scientists think that the first mammals appeared as a variety of little guys, almost under the feet of the dinosaurs. They describe them as like mice, beavers, or other rodent-like creatures, eking out a very different lifestyle (an "ecological niche") concurrent with the reign of the dinosaurs.

Everything in the picture we just came up with supports that same picture with no reference to, or need to refer to, absolute time scales and so-called "evolution." The Scripture says (with no description of how, actually) they were created ("brought forth by the waters") in Creation-day five.

The scientists also, by the way, believe that amphibians appear here at this point in the Creation outline or scheme of things, just as Genesis outlines. And, as we've already discussed, they also believe the insects appeared in the order and place that Genesis says. That's quite a bit of matching up that no one had noticed before.

And what about the rest of the verse, the third and last of this creation-set (we could call "21c")? Well, it is after this— after insects, dinosaurs, and mammals—that scientists think the first birds appeared. So, naturally, that's exactly what shows up next in verse 21c, the birds!

This time *"and every winged fowl"* is definitely about birds. Why do I say so? Well, recall that when we were talking about the "fowl" in verse 20, I made the point that the *owph,* in that context, referred to insects instead of birds. Here, in verse 21, the *owph* comes with a companion, the word *kanaph,* which means "feather" and "wing" (especially a bird wing), and an "extremity" (again, the descriptive detail matches a wing on a bird, not an insect). I have no doubt that here Genesis very deliberately emphasizes the difference, essentially saying, "every bird-winged, feathered (flying) thing," as opposed to the earlier "things with wings that may fly" in verse 20.

OK. That tells you where the dinosaurs have been hidden all these years. And it clears up one of the more popular criticisms in scientific circles regarding the timing of birds in the Creation account. Now we are ready for something else.

Remember our discussion of *miyn? Miyn,* translated "after his kind," is the conservative genetic principle, designating an immutable and unchanging species (or genera or other grouping of species), which was carefully proclaimed about all the higher plant kinds (species?). *Miyn,* with *zera,* sets forth the functional principles of DNA and proscribes (rules against) evolution. Remember, also, the rather surprising and curious exception? Remember that *miyn* was not, to all appearances, applied to the simplest, lower levels of plant life? That exception suggests there is a possibility, I pointed out, that unless God was just not being clear or completely precise, that *miyn* did not apply to those lower levels of plants. From that we speculated that some simpler forms of life were not immutable. They could mutate; they could change beyond the variability of races; and they could give rise to new species and "evolve," perhaps, in these days since the Creation. Well, the same bombshell is dropped in our laps again! There is no "after his kind," no statement of *miyn,* in verse 20. None of those first, simplest lowest levels of animal life, teeming and swarming in the shallow waters in verse 20, are specifically included under the conservative principles of *miyn.* That includes those creatures that we have interpreted to be the insects, the first *owph!* In verse 21b, we see *miyn,* "after his kind," given twice. All the *ramas* creatures, the small, but higher levels of life from the waters, are *miyn.* All the birds, the *owph kanaph* are *miyn.* So it looks like we are expressly not told that insects, bacteria, and such simpler forms of animal life—indeed, those types that overrun the earth in nearly infinite numbers and varieties today and that seem to defy all our attempts at using antibiotics and insecticides to control them (by mutating and adapting, even evolving resistant new types, we are told by science)—are bound by the Law of Conservation, if that is what *miyn* is!

Is this another signpost? Has Genesis revealed something to us that science, even as prone to embracing evolution as it is, is just beginning to realize? Did Genesis actually give us forewarning that our best inventions and technologies cannot control insects and disease organisms because they are free to evade us genetically?

Did this ancient Creation account, written before anyone knew there were bacteria and viruses, and before anyone ever comprehended the extent of the insects' variety and numbers, tell us that they are not bound by the "no evolution" law of *miyn?*

The facts certainly seem indisputable. Diseases, like HIV, malaria, and tuberculosis, and insects like mosquitoes and ticks, seem to reinvent themselves so quickly, they outflank us again and again, eluding every miracle cure and every eradication program we devise. Within years they seem to just laugh at DDT and penicillin. Suppose the plagues and the "beasts" we read of in the Revelation, and are told will devastate humankind during the Tribulation period, are plagues of diseases and insects ("minibeast"). Suppose they are species that are not constrained by *miyn*. Suppose they are, by God's own design, quite "lawfully" able to mutate and evolve beyond our ability to defend ourselves. Then do we have a signpost here, pointing out the very "how" of the future foretold in Revelation? Whether it is or not, it is certainly a clue, which, if we are reading it right, the world should pay attention to.

Scientists, as many Christian apologists like to claim, have never seen a real case of species evolution. Well, that's not quite true. While there are no absolutely demonstrable cases of higher species evolving, there are increasingly numerous instances of what appear to be evolving viruses, bacteria, and insects—and some plants, perhaps. How we can define what's happening, of course, depends a lot on how one defines "species." There are also a number of very contrived (unnatural conditions are imposed) experiments in laboratories that have apparently produced new species in such insects as fruit flies. And, as we've just said, it looks very much like some insects in the natural world have very significantly changed their habitats, resistance to insecticides, and so on. So the evolutionists do have some pretty credible evidence for evolution, but only at these lowest levels of life. But that's hardly a refutation of Genesis, especially if we are correct in our interpretation here that the lower levels are free from *miyn!*

If we are correct, I think the evolutionary theologians' exuberance should surely be tempered, if not downright discouraged. It appears to me the Genesis account "wins" this debate, and what they have managed to eke out of their studies so far, only continue to build the case for Genesis and the Creator!

Now, I have one last rather intriguing point to bring out about verse 21 (21*a*, actually. When we were discussing *miyn* above, I omitted to point out one more thing to you. In verse 21*a*, the dinosaurs are not directly put under *miyn,* either! That's quite a surprise, I think. Perhaps it is an artifact of (created by) my division of the verse. But two things might make us wonder whether that is the right conclusion. First, the split of the verse is reasonable, logical, and works well with the two separate create-verbs. Second, dinosaurs never seem to stop being a remarkable, exceptional event in the Creation, right from their *bara* creation.

Indeed, there are even more exceptions to be noted, as we move forward to verse 22 and the conclusion of Creation-day five.

> Genesis 1:22 *And God blessed them, saying, Be fruitful, and multiply, and fill the waters in the seas, and let fowl multiply in the earth.*

This is rather interesting. It is here that God pronounces His first blessing upon His creations. It is here that He issues His first command to all His creation to be fruitful and to spread across the globe. We don't see dinosaurs today, but the fossil record certainly shows that they, perhaps like no other form of life, fulfilled that command. Except, of course, for the indomitable insects and bacteria types. But it is the dinosaurs, for sure, that are the most dramatic and attention-grabbing and the most mysterious of all the Creation (other than man, of course). Dinosaurs "owned" the earth for an incredibly long time, if we are to believe the best evidence of our eyes and shovels, as they reveal the apparent length, breadth, depth, and volume of their fossil remains. But then to all appearances they totally, almost instantly, disappear. None remain. But their image and their mystery, still disproportionately tantalizes and fascinates the modern world.

Of course, that fascination and disproportionate influence that dinosaurs continue to exert, especially upon our children, is exactly the reason for the title of this book. I believe that because children are so constantly aware of dinosaurs nowadays, we really need to reassure them the Bible does explicitly account for them. And when we do, isn't all the more fascinating to see the rather special treatment they get in the Creation account? Now wait until you see the special treatment they get in just a few more verses!

CHAPTER FIVE

WHAT ABOUT MAN?
WHAT ABOUT ADAM?

The verse which opens the sixth and last *yowm* of the Creation account of Genesis is really rather unique. You wouldn't know it at first reading; it sounds very much like some other verses.

> Genesis 1:24 *And God said, Let the earth bring forth the living creature after his kind, cattle, and creeping thing, and beast of the earth after his kind and it was so.*

Compare that to verse 11:

> Genesis 1:11 *And God said, Let the earth bring forth grass, the herb yielding seed, and . . .*

And to verse 20:

> Genesis 1:20 *And God said, Let the waters bring forth abundantly the moving creature . . .*

Each starts out with the same language, "Let the [something] bring forth. . . ." Wouldn't you expect, then, that each is a translation of the same language in the original Hebrew Scriptures? Well, truth is, they aren't. The similarity is only in our English version, not in the Hebrew. And as always, I think the original Scripture is far more interesting than our English interpretation, which, in this case, is quite a compromise translation. It works all right, I suppose, for some purposes, but loses some intriguing information that we should regain for ours. Let's see what we lost in getting it into English, and we might recover from the Hebrew.

Verse 11, you'll recall, recounts the origins of plants. We didn't even look at the verb when we studied verse 11. We were mostly concerned with sorting out just what things the earth was commanded to "bring forth," and especially with the first, with *deshe*. We found that the first plant life produced was not grass, but the simplest of the various plant forms, such as algae. That was what *deshe* was, we concluded, not grass as the English translations always conclude.

What was the verb, the word that provided the power or action to the commandment in verse 11? What was it that the earth was to do that our King James Version translated as "bring forth *deshe*"? The verb was *dasha*. When we search out the meaning of the word, we find that *dasha* is an extraordinarily good fit. It's practically a verbal synonym for *deshe*; it basically says "sprout," or "grow green." It's almost like there is some of *deshe* in *dasha*. We can see a clear predictive or defining quality in *dasha* that looks ahead to the nature of the creations that come of it. It adds to our interpretation and understanding of what was being done that Creation-day.

Now, looking at verse 20, we find we have a very similar situation. We've already examined the verb that denoted the action, which described what the waters were to do to fulfill what our King James Version rendered as "bring forth." In verse 20, we were being told about the first animal life, the *sherets,* those tiny microscopic, and nearly microscopic, life forms that now animate every drop of pond water. And the verb, here, is *sharats. Sharats,* too, with its definition of "swarm" and "teem," is practically a verbal synonym for *sherets. Sharats,* too, seems to essentially anticipate, to look ahead at the nature of the *sherets* it "brings forth"! Doing that, it surely helps us correctly translate and interpret the content of verse 20.

Should we look for something similar going on in verse 24? Will the very verb used help us expand or improve our sense of what is being done in Creation-day six? Verse 24 tells us to look for some "living creature." There's no surprise in that, considering where we are in the account. We are expressly told that these living creatures are all going to be "after his kind," which we've come to understand means that the creatures are both higher-level animal types and governed by the conservative genetic principle of *miyn.* That's no surprise either.

Then following this introduction, which tells us what is going to happen in this creation set in general, we are given a list of three animal types, or categories. That is little surprising. It's the first time we've been told "God created some things" and then had a list provided to fill in the details. Previously, we've gone directly into the list. This time, we have a first phrase (the translator could have even treated it as a separate verse) that seems to be making some extra point, putting in some extra emphasis about these particular "living creatures" and their kinds *(miyn).* And when we finally get the three-item list, only one of the three (according to our translators) is something you and I would readily recognize: cattle. The other two types of creatures are "creeping things," and "beasts of the earth"! I have no idea just reading that of what those are. But I look forward to finding out just what they are, don't you? In fact, I actually have no intention of accepting the translators' word for "cattle," either!

But the question we're involved with right now is: No matter what the creatures are, will our verb in verse 24 include in itself anything predictive about them; will it help us translate what they are, or come to understand better just what is being done in this sixth Creation-day? Will the verb add any new information to help us translate with more precision or certainty, or better understand the Creator's purposes?

Our English translation simply reads, *"Let the earth bring forth . . ."* I certainly don't expect that a deeper search into the Hebrew will reveal a verb that says essentially, "Let the earth sprout (greenish) cattle, and so forth . . ." or "Let the earth teem and swarm (tiny merry) cattle, and so forth. . . ." I'm very sure that this "averaged out," or "compromise," translation "Let . . . bring forth" is concealing something else. What is in verse 24 is not the same as was in verses 11 and 20.

The Hebrew verse 24 actually uses the verb *yatsa*. At first blush, *yatsa* does translate into a sort of "Let [the earth] bring forth." Its common rendering elsewhere in the Scriptures is "to go out," "to go forth," or "to proceed to." If you look closely, however, each of those definitions shares another very interesting implication, as I see it. One very respected authority (Brown-Driver-Briggs) explicitly includes that implication in several of its definitions: "to proceed toward something;" "to go forth with purpose;" "to go forth for a result." In other words, *yatsa* says "do these things—toward some greater goal with a further purpose or for a future result." I've read ahead, of course, and so I know why this is so interesting, but let me take you there step-by-step, relying on the meaning within *yatsa*, and not just on hindsight.

Let's look again at *dasha*. *Dasha,* we said, says "sprout" or "produce" (even "germinate") something "plants." For *dasha,* producing green plants is as far as it goes. Making green plants is what it is doing; that's the full program; that's the whole objective; it's the end result. Likewise, look at *sharats.* For *sharats,* the action and program is to lead to, or result in, swarms of tiny living animals in the swampy waters of the earth and the hordes of insects to expand the animal domain into the other media—land and sky. It went no further. When higher animals were to be created, a new verb and creative power was introduced. The Scripture was very careful, in fact, to make sure we saw that limitation; that *sharats* was confined to the tiny creatures of verse 20, and to make sure we didn't mistakenly carry its action or connotations on into verse 21, and its very different kinds of life.

Yatsa doesn't carry the same sort of anticipation as did the first two verbs. It doesn't say "green" or "plant;" it doesn't include any particular "animal-ness" that could point us toward what the "moving creatures" that follow it are. *Yatsa* carries a far more subtle anticipation or predictive connotation about the creatures to next be "brought forth." It tells us that it has a further down-the-road purpose involved. *Yatsa* suggests we should look beyond just the "living creatures" themselves, to fully realize what the Creator is doing. *Yatsa* tells us there is some defined end or specific purpose(s) further on in the process, which the Creator wants us to recognize.

Let me give you another illustration of what I mean by this further down-the-road-purpose thing. Consider how similar words, or even identical words, can convey such "extra" meanings. If I say, "He grew tall," "tall" is the full and inevitable outcome of that meaning of "grow." That's more like *dasha*. But, if I say, "He grew wiser," that's more a *yatsa* shade of meaning. "Wiser" is a further—even higher or more noble—outcome, a down-the-road purpose of what he did (say, he studied long and hard) in order to "grow wiser." Most of us, for instance, go to college in order to get a good job. We expect our going to college to "produce" a degree, but that's not our ultimate end, our *yatsa* end. We really want to produce a further-down-the-road objective in our plan, like a good-paying job or the opportunity to save lives with our medical training (you became a doctor). That's more like the meaning of *yatsa*.

I believe the use of *yatsa* in verse 24 is intended to indicate something more than just the production of the three types, or categories, of life that follow in its list. There are at least two possibilities, two further, or superior goals, that I can think of. As we carefully interpret the next three types of life that are *yatsa'd,* it appears as if the earth (planet) is now moving toward the completion of the whole project, the system of the final ecology, the full "web of life." That may be the goal being implied by *yatsa;* finishing the natural ecology. Another interpretation might be that *yatsa* is anticipating the final reason, the ultimate objective in all the works of creation, which the Bible repeatedly tells of: the creation of mankind.

If we go back to our imaginary scenario, where you are preparing a grand estate for a very important "first family," I can illustrate my meaning. From the very bare-soils beginning, step-by-step, you've been getting the grounds ready. Each step along the way, you stop and let the workmen achieve your directives. You let them get the finishing touches in place and be ready for the next stage. Before you launch the next step, you inspect the work and make sure it's all good, just as you want it. You make sure that the system works so far, before you proceed toward the end of your program. You introduce fish when the waters are ready and when there's a supply of food to keep them; you plant the roses when the soil is rich and fertile; you bring in the bees when the orchard is ready, and so on. It's a very long and complex process when you start from absolute scratch. When it's finally just about done and you're ready to put the finishing touches that this family will interact with and care about the most, you need to think very carefully about the future residents and consider what they personally will need and enjoy. You select the pets, horses, breeds of cattle, and whatever other "beast of the earth" they might want, *yatsa* fashion. If they like quarter horses, you get them quarter horses. If they like poodles, and not mastiffs, you get poodles—anticipating their interests exactly.

The use of *yatsa,* with this extra sense of attention to a future, final objective of the present last works, might be an intentional affirmation—indeed, the first such affirmation of many in the Bible—that the whole of the Creation is by design and for the purpose of creating, establishing, and nurturing mankind. That's my theory, anyway.

Let's go ahead and learn what we can about the "living creatures," and whether they fit either hypothesis about *yatsa.* Let's see what things are being "*yatsa'd;* what is (rather, what are) "the living creature(s) after his kind."

There's no great mystery about the language that is translated "living creature;" we've seen it all before. The "living" comes from *chay* (pronounced "ka-ee," remember?). "Living" is pretty much its meaning. Something *chay* is something alive, although as we noted before, *chay* has such an emphasis on life, it almost requires an exclamation point (life!) to be sufficiently translated into English. "Creature" is from another word we've already encountered, as well—*nephesh. Nephesh* makes it totally clear that we're considering animals, as it refers to a collection of uniquely animal qualities, such as "breath," "life in the blood," and soulish qualities, such as mind, appetites, the pursuit of happiness (satisfying appetites). "After his kind," of course, is from *miyn.*

Now, what about the list of three "kinds" of life? It's obvious they are detailing at least the range of "living creatures" being created, not saying exactly what they all are and defining and clarifying

"Hey Mom, What About Dinosaurs?"

what sorts of animals they all are. That is, all the "cattle, and creeping thing, and beast of the earth" are the *chay nephesh* being *yatsa'd*.

The first in the list, "cattle," as we've said before, seems simple enough. If you were just a casual reader, you'd accept that at face value, wouldn't you? Well, as is too often the case, they "got ya again." Cattle was a pretty poor pick from a number of meanings available and is definitely misleading. It is far too narrow an interpretation. The Hebrew word is *behemah*. *Behemah* is indeed often translated as cattle by our old English scholars, but it really represents a very large class of animals. Translating it as simply cattle, especially in this situation (the Creation account of all life), is about like translating chickens for *owph* (remember verse 20, and how *owph* actually stands for "all things that fly"?). The *behemah* are a collection of all kinds of large quadrupeds (four-legged animals). *Behemah* are not all of the large quadrupeds, but they include a great many of them, both wild and untamable, and those which we have often domesticated, such as cows, horses, and goats. You'd come closer to comprehending the *behemah* class if you think of all the various grazers and herd animals we see in the plains of Africa. Not just cattle.

The translator's next language, however—"and creeping thing"—is probably an even more misleading translation for us, especially the way we interpret those words today. "Creeping thing" ranks right up there with substituting whales for dinosaurs, in my opinion. Once again, the problem is mostly a product of cultural differences and changes in the English language between 1600 England and today. In the 1600's, in fact, "creeping thing" probably wasn't too bad a translation, as best I've been able to tell, but for today it's way off.

The real burden of defining these particular creeping creatures falls on the word *remes*. It is what the King James people decided made category two "creeping." In the context of verse 24, the Creation-*yowm* of the last and highest animals, we have the large mammals, including the four-footed beasts of the plains and forests and all the beasts that men now domesticate. So it is more than reasonable to expect this next group should be something other than creeping (if that suggests lizards or something under the house, to you). We might expect the *remes* animals (that is, *remes chay nephesh*) to be another whole class of animals. In fact, using the word *remes*, we find the Scripture is really talking about fast, not creeping! *Remes* can be interpreted as quick, such as a lizard or a bobcat, and is better read as swift and fleet-footed, when applied to larger four-footed beasts. Paired with *chay* as it is, we have a lot of life and vitality, and the swiftness of foot in a quadruped mammal is anything but creeping—except and unless we understand creeping as stealth and stalking.

If we interpret our *chay remes* in this way, we just might have found the other half of the ecology of the world, the "balancing" half of the whole animal ecology. We may have just now accounted for the creation of the predators. Here we have the perfect connotations for cheetahs, lions, wolves, and, perhaps, even such creatures as the saber-tooth tigers. It's debatable, to be sure, but still very reasonable.

If we accept the analysis we just made of *yatsa* and the speculation that one of the outcomes or purposes being forecast by that verb is completing the ecology, the predators and grazers are both absolutely necessary, at least for the ecology we of our world today. Some people don't believe that predators existed before "the Fall." But lacking any direct statement about that, any indication of a new set of creations (such as all the predators) in the seventh Creation-day, and any proof that mere physical death of an animal or plant is evil, they have a ways to go to make their case. And I think we have a good case for our interpretation.

Another interpreter, Dr. Hugh Ross, however, considers these two (Hebrew) categories as those animals that are easy to domesticate *(behemah)* and those that are not *(remes)*. And he makes a good argument. But interestingly enough, he, too, was responding to the sense of greater and future purposes implied in *yatsa*, which I've argued for, but he was taking a different (and narrower) interpretive perspective, looking only at their utility to man rather than the whole ecology as I have.

The third item in the list, the "beast of the earth," is probably there mostly for inclusiveness and emphasis, making sure we understand that all the higher animals are His handiwork, rather than for any other reason. The Hebrew Scripture behind "beast of the earth" is a repeated use of the more inclusive *chay*, such as "all the living things!," and a repeat of *erets*, which does mean "earth," but in this context the word adds the flavor of terra firma, and field or wilderness. It's much as if God said, "I created the beasts of paddock and field; the beasts of prey and grace; indeed, I created all the beasts that walk upon the land." In fact, earth *(erets)* is used twice in verse 24. The first time ("Let the earth bring forth") it seems to be more in the sense of "all the earth," such as when we say, "In all God's green earth"—planet-wide. The second use of *erets* perhaps intends a less grandiose connotation, suggesting an interpretation like "on the face of the land." That may be the actual reason for the final phrase, "beast of the earth."

Putting all this discussion together, I would be very comfortable if the Scripture read like this:

> Genesis 1:24 *And God said, Let my earth now bring forth all the species I have designed, the beasts of the field (some of which man will domesticate; others he will hunt), the predators (magnificently designed and ultimately vital to the balanced ecology the Creator designed), and all the animals of the land (as opposed to those of*

the waters in the previous Creation-day), each after its own kind. And it was so!

Verse 25 is another one that repeats a pattern we've seen before and uses some similar language. Indeed, it goes back over verse 24 in much the same way verse 12 went back over verse 11. That's interesting. Do you recall what we discovered about verse 12, when we dug more deeply into its message? For one thing, it actually clarified any ambiguity there might have been in verse 11. So we need to see if that's the purpose of verse 25. We want to see whether it's more than just a literary or dramatic technique to draw the curtain closed on this, the next to the last act of the drama of Creation. As regards literary style, it certainly can work that way, like the curtain between acts. In this "midday" break in His work, God reflects upon what He has done to that point and says, "It is good." You can almost hear Him drawing in a deep breath, anticipating the next lump of clay to be put upon His potter's wheel. But, there is more in verse 25 than that.

Genesis 1:25 And God made the beast of the earth after his kind, and cattle after their kind, and every thing that creepeth upon the earth after his kind and God saw that it was good.

As you see, the verse does sum things up. It repeats the list of three, it reaffirms that God did indeed make them all, and it adds the remark that He was very satisfied—that as He looked upon the landscape, it was excellent in His sight; it was exactly what He wanted it to be. But we mustn't stop there. We shouldn't even leave the "saw that it was good" alone, just accepting it as it appears. I'll show you why in a moment.

First, let's look into the original Hebrew, which our English King James Version translates "God made." We are no longer working with the *yatsa* of the original "Let the earth produce . . ." in verse 24.

In this verse 25 recap, we find the Scripture uses the creating-verb *asah*, the verb, which says He "fashioned," "designed," or "appointed" these species; and not *bara*, the verb that says "from scratch," as it did when He created the universe and dinosaurs. *Asah* definitely implies less *"ex nihilo"* (from nothing) and more *"ex materia"* (from existing stuff), to use terms that theologians like.

Second, something else happened that you don't see in the English. The first "earth" comes from *erets*, again. It reads, essentially, "He fashioned all the beasts found upon His green earth." The second "earth," however, is from a new word we've not seen yet: *adamah*. If that sounds like "Adam," it should; Adam is transliterated from *adam*, which is the root of *adamah*. This use of *adamah* in this review of the first verse, certainly seems to affirm the validity of the distinction I drew before between "earth as planet" and "earth as soil, ground." *Adamah* means ground or soil only. So verse 25 reiterates that point and serves to clarify a few other things. It emphasizes by using *erets* the first time, *adamah* the second time, and by the three repetitions of *miyn*, the loud and clear message that upon all His earth He created the higher animal species, completely under the anti-evolutionary genetic principle of *miyn*. These are His "kinds," as this verse says, "Let there be no question about it"

I am led to wonder why the explicitness and loud emphasis on this. It's possible He anticipates our playing around with the various species, trying to "improve" the breeds, and He wants us to know that that is neither evolution, nor creating anything new that He did not create. Our animal husbandry is only exploiting the genetic variation He built into the original. It might also be telling us what some would deny on theological grounds—that the predators and the prey are part of His original design as well. They are no recent evolution, or kinds, appearing since the work of Creation-day six.

But aside from that, there is still more for us to pay attention to. The verse concludes, just as we've seen many other verses conclude, with "and God saw that it was good." That statement, I'm about to show you, is another one of those many phrases, simple little things in the Scriptures, that we tend to just slide right past, never paying them serious attention. We shouldn't do that. The Lord was not being an overbearing parent when He said, "meditate upon my word, constantly." He was telling us that it is always to our advantage to study His every word. Meditating on "God saw that it was good" definitely yields more precious insight.

First, let's look at what *"and God saw that it was good"* is in the original Hebrew: "God" is from *Elohiym*. *Elohiym* is God the Creator before He became known to men and established a relationship with them. Once God established a relationship, as He did with Adam, He is called Jehovah in the Scriptures. So here, before that relationship is established, we have *Elohiym* looking over His works. The word "saw" is translated from *ra-ah*. *Ra-ah* is much more than just "to see;" it is actually "to inspect," "to consider," or "to observe." This is "seeing" with a purpose; taking a long, intense and purposeful look at things; this is "observing" closely how it all works; this is "inspecting." The sense of this phrase is that He inspected the end product, the result of what He had commanded be accomplished.

This is the work of Jesus, if John 1:1–3 refers to Jesus, as is commonly believed. It is also the result of a long-time process, if you accept the translations and thesis of this book and the conclusion of science (sans evolution)—that the creation processes took far more than 144 hours.

Continuing our detailed analysis of that phrase *"and God saw that it was good,"* we find that "that" is from *kiy*. *Kiy* best translates as "because," "since," or "when." *Kiy* is a word expressing a causal connection, and it is not being very well translated by a simple "that," in English.

"It was" is added by the translators; it is not in the original Scripture.

"Good" is from *towb*. *Towb* means "good," "excellent," "appropriate," and "of benefit," as in "to the best benefit or welfare of someone." It strongly implies that God saw (or concluded) that the works were "good for" and not just "good."

So, *Elohiym ra-ah kiy towb* can be interpreted as a stronger statement than "God saw that it was good." It can be better read to say that God inspected it, examined it, observed it, and with His infinite capacity and thoroughness, He determined it was all that He planned and all that He required. This, again, gives support to that interpretation of *yatsa*, that it is pointing ahead to a greater end and purpose than just the immediate creatures we discussed earlier.

Have you ever built a house or had one built? A house is built by many workmen, by a variety of subcontractors, each of whom must follow the plans of the designer-architect and meet the specifications of the "builder's codes." Each time a part of the job is finished, from foundation to framing, to plumbing, to wiring, to insulating, to roofing, the project is inspected. It doesn't go forward and the next step isn't taken until the last step is inspected and found satisfactory and deemed perfect for your benefit and welfare.

That's what *Elohiym ra-ah kiy towb* seems to describe. If we look back through the first twenty-five verses of the Creation project, we find there are twelve times that we are told of how the work is going. Six times, however, we are only told that whatever was to be created had indeed become, or happened, precisely as commanded (*hayah*, "it was so"!). The other six times we are told that God Himself has inspected the work and has been satisfied that the results were "excellent" and appropriate for what was coming next.

We learn something rather interesting when we look at how and where the two different "it was so" and "it was good" conclusions are presented. I've put all twelve into a verse-by-verse analysis in Table 1.

Table 1

Creation Comandments and Comments or Conclusions

Verse	Creating-Verb	Creating		Conclusion
1.	bara	absolute create	heavens and earth	
2.	hayah	let it be/become	light	
3.				hayah...it manifested thus
4.				Elohiym ra-ah kiy tobe
4.	badal	divided	light and dark	
6.	hayah	let there be	sky	
6.	hayah, badal,	let it divide	waters from waters	
7.	asah	design, appoint	sky, heavens	
7.				hayah
9.	qavah	look/wait for the waters to gather		
9.	ra-ah	observe, behold dry land appear		
9.				hayah
10.				Elohiym r-h kiy tobe
11.	dasha	let the earth grow	plant life	
11.				hayah
12.	yatsa	earth produce for purposes		
12.				Elohiym ra-ah kiy tobe
14.	hayah	let there be	stars, constellations	
15.	hayah	let them be	cheering lights	
15.				hayah
16.	asah	design, appoint	(sun?), moon	
18.				Elohiym ra-ah kiy tobe
20.	sharats	let the waters produce abundantly	animal life, and insects	
21.	bara	absolute create	dinosaurs	
21.	sharats	waters produced	higher species of animal and birds	
21.				Elohiym ra-ah kiy tobe
24.	yatsa	earth produce for purposes	higher species, beasts, predators, all land animals	
24.				hayah
25.				Elohiym ra-ah kiy tobe

As you can see, whenever there is a "let it be," or "let something (else) produce" statement, wherever *hayah* is used, the conclusion is reported by that same verb as, "indeed, *hayah!*"—indeed, it manifested just so, precisely that way. *Elohiym ra-ah kiy towb,* occurs when major stages are completed, such as when all of the animal species are created or the waters have receded into a sea and the dry land has emerged. Even more interesting, perhaps, is that it occurs when other agents seem to be entailed in the production or creation work. Such agents might be Jesus, or they might be natural physical processes (say, plate tectonics, nuclear fusion, or even chemical reactions), or natural laws (like gravity or entropy), which seem to be being expressed in "let the earth . . ." or "let the waters . . ." But here is something even more interesting: *Elohiym* never *ra-ah's* a creation work after *bara,* the create-verb that definitely says, "God Himself created" and has no need to inspect His own hand's work. That's a powerful bit of coincidence to say the least.

Verse 26 in Genesis 1, starts the last chapter of the Creation account—not the last Creation-day, but the last chapter. This is the big one. This is "man." But be aware, this is only where the chapter begins. The full account of man is not finished here in Genesis 1, and before this book is done, we'll need to go beyond the actual creation account, as we've been defining it thus far. Genesis 1 is about the whole history of Creation, but only on the physical, natural plane. Man is something more, as you and I know. Man includes a spiritual nature and a mind that has no equal in the rest of the creation, and which remains unaccounted and unexplained in Genesis 1. At best, there is only one verse that hints of that extra dimension to man. We'll need to look at some significant verses in Genesis 2 and 3 to understand the rest of the story, to understand the fullness of the Creation. But right now, let's just see what else there is for us in the rest of Genesis 1.

What About Man? What About Adam?

> Genesis 1:26 *And God said, Let us make man in our image, after our likeness: and let them have dominion over the fish of the sea, and over the fowl of the air, and over the cattle, and over all the earth, and over every creeping thing that creepeth upon the earth.*
> Genesis 1:27 *So God created man in his own image, in the image of God created he him; male and female created he them.*

The first thing we should look at here is the create-verbs. What we find in these two verses together is going to be rather intriguing.

In the first verse, "make" comes from *asah*. The Scripture we just read as, *"Let us make man in our image,"* may be much better understood as saying, "Let us fashion or design man in our own image." We've already learned that *asah* is a word that means less than absolute, hands-on, creating out of nothing, but it definitely means more than "Let it happen," or "Let it come to be according to this plan and purpose." That refined definition begins to pay off quite a dividend when we delve further into the verse. The Scripture says, "Let us *asah adam* in our own *tselem*. *Adam* and *tselem* are two words well worth studying and understanding more precisely their definitions.

The word "image" comes from *tselem*, which very definitely talks about "image" or "shape;" in fact, the word often doubles for "idol" or "carved image." Thus the two words, *asah* and *tselem*, really fit well together, don't they? God says, "Let us fashion man like this...." He obviously has a special model in mind.

The word *adam* is translated variously as "man," "mankind," or "men." It's not really a very particular or discriminating word in Hebrew. It could be that it originally meant, as implied in the "kind" *(miyn)* of mankind, the human species. Then as time passed, because we like to have proper names for individuals, it became rendered as a name, "Adam." Whatever the case, the more important points for us at this time are: 1) that *adam* can mean just "human species" or "human beings" and, 2) that the Hebrew Scripture uses exactly *adam,* here, with no additional modification of the word or form. In just one more verse that will no longer be true, *adam* will be replaced by *ha-adam*—a very significant change.

For now, let's just continue with this verse and take up the next phrase, "after our likeness." T*selem,* as we've seen, is a thing, although it may be a rather abstract and non-material thing, such as a phantom or illusion. Still, it's just a set, immutable thing. But after saying "Let us fashion man in our *tselem*-image," the Scripture goes on to tell us about a second goal of the *asah*-design—about "likeness." *Demuwth* is what the King James Version translated "likeness." For years, I must confess that translation never made much sense to me. I never felt I really understood what it meant. I was still confused about what God did or what He meant to tell us about ourselves. I really didn't see the difference between image and likeness. I finally got the answer when I realized that *demuwth* is not an object idea, not a thing like a picture-likeness or figurine. *Demuwth* is a process, or adverbial concept; it expresses a relationship or manner of being.

If we look at the root of the word, we discover that *demuwth,* as much as anything, says that man shall be like, behave like, think like, or even make himself like, God. I've come to understand this to mean that we, unlike other creatures of the Creation, are designed to try to be like God Himself. That's what this verse is saying. Doesn't that make sense? One of the most consistent teachings in the New Testament is exactly that. Paul, especially, says it again and again in so many ways: *"be transformed"*; *"have the mind of Christ . . . not carnal and behaving like mere men"*; *"Imitate me just as I also imitate Christ"* (Rom. 12.2; I Cor.2: 16, 3:3, and 11:1 NKJV). Paul repeatedly said, "Do not behave like mere men, like mere *adam!*"

Now consider verse 27. It continues the subject, saying that "God created . . . created . . . created. . . ." Three times it says "created." It makes this distinction very clear. In verse 26, God has told us His intent and His design (*asah* in *tselem* and *demuwth*) in making man, or mankind. Then in verse 27, we are told God actually *bara*-created man (not *asah*-fashioned or delegated), both male and female, in His image (*tselem*, and not, at this time, *demuwth*). This *bara*, remember, is the "absolutely, from-scratch, like-nothing-ever-done-before" create (see Exodus 34:10 for an example of "first time ever"), hands-on by God himself. No intermediaries; no other agents. This use of *bara*, after the initial *asah adam*, must be telling us something of importance, so hold on to that point (call it point number one). As we noted in Chapter Four, *bara* is only used in three instances: The absolute beginning of everything (the "Big Whoosh"), dinosaurs, and mankind.

Point number two concerns the fact that, following this "hands-on" *bara*, we immediately shift to a new form of *adam* in the Hebrew—from now on it will be *ha-adam*. This *"ha,"* when attached to any word throughout the Scriptures, linguistically indicates the touch of God on whatever that word is representing. This is a very important connection often overlooked by translators. *Ha* will attach to waters, heavens, beasts, soil, everything, and anything (even men!) that God has touched, or is otherwise brought into a sanctified standing by His use or concern. It's almost as if when God's eyes turn toward something, it becomes *"ha."* This *adam*, touched by God's *bara* creation, will be *ha-adam* from now on, with only a few very telling exceptions.

But here is point number three: This *"ha"* does not attach to the "male" and "female" after the second and third *bara* verbs. It leads me to suspect that we have here another case where we should split a verse into two. In fact, after studying the original language and reflecting on the whole content of the account—what it says in terms of the physical creation and comparing that to the "spiritual creation account" of Genesis 2—I think we not only have two sentences, but one is fully parenthetical, sort of a "footnote." Verse 27 should read this way:

Genesis 1:27a *"So God created mankind in His own image."*

Here's the point: In verse 26, God says He is planning to make mankind (*adam*) in His own *tselem* (image) and *demuwth* (desiring to be like Him). This parenthetical verse says "So God created mankind (*ha-adam,* the one that has that *demuwth*) in His own image." The details of that transformation, *adam* into *ha-adam,* are given in Genesis 2.

Genesis 1:27b *In His own image He created the males and the females.*

We will pursue this matter much further in the next chapter, when we get to the Scriptures that will let us make the most of it. As I just noted a little earlier, Genesis 1 is only intended to provide a brief outline of all the Creation in natural physical terms and man is definitely a part of that. He has a very natural physical body and a natural place in the Creation ecology, and mankind was created just as all kinds of living things were—so Genesis 1 says. But verse 26 also tells us that there was more to the plan right from the beginning, as far as mankind was concerned. The above parenthetical statement of verse 27a preserves that point, allowing accurate flow of the Genesis 1 narration, but reminding us that there is more to come, and pointing ahead to the fact man will be made more than physical man. That done, verse 27b gets back to the account at hand.

As we continue our study of the account at hand in verse 27, we also realize that the three *bara* verbs are applied very precisely to, and only to, *tselem,* the concrete shape-image word. That's point number four. There are two opportunities, in fact, for the account to be perfectly clear about what is being done, and both times the *bara* verb is applied to *tselem,* and not to the more spiritual, or more behavioral, "likeness" of *demuwth. Demuwth* is clearly left out of this immediate, concrete statement of mankind's physical creation. *Demuwth* was only mentioned once in verse 26 in the "design-intended," or "appointed-purpose," part of the description of the Creation.

The answers we may really want, regarding our spiritual nature and our special relationship with the Creator, must wait until we reach Genesis 2, even Genesis 3.

The rest of Genesis 1 will only tell us about our physical selves and our place in the rest of the Creation, where we are in the context of it, the "ecology," as scientists would say. Verse 26 begins that task when it continues:

> Genesis 1:26 . . . *and let them have dominion over the fish of the sea, and over the fowl of the air, and over every creeping thing that creepeth upon the earth.*

There are both some answers and some mysteries there. You'll notice that the verse says that the new mankind is going to have dominion over all the rest of the animals upon the earth. That's what it says, right? Or is it? Let's look a little more closely. We know that dominion means "to have full power over and use of, and be unthreatened and unchallenged by" those you have dominion over. If that's the meaning, then it appears that, in the Genesis account of the ecological order, mankind is the real "king of the jungle." Except for some very fascinating exceptions. The first is the dinosaurs! The list did not include the dinosaurs. Was that an oversight? Or should we assume dinosaurs are among the "every creeping thing"? I don't think so.

To begin with, as I continually point out, God is not careless, but very precise. So consider the following facts. First, dinosaurs are quite exceptional in the Creation list, not to mention our present-day psyches. They are so exceptional that they, of all living

"Hey Mom, What About Dinosaurs?"

things, are the only ones, other than man, specifically *bara*-created. Is it likely they should be overlooked? The *behemah* and *chay remes* are not.

Second, not only are dinosaurs not explicitly listed, but in that phrase *"every creeping thing that creepeth,"* there may be an explicit "not dinosaurs." How's that? Well, "creeping thing" (*chay remes*), as we've already seen, appears to designate the predators, the dangerous species. The additional "that creepeth" (from *ramas*) is rather redundant, unless it should either be intended to contrast with the "heavy, ponderous, frightening" motion originally ascribed to the dinosaurs, or intended to designate "kinds that still walk" upon the earth!

That last interpretation would suggest a third reason that dinosaurs were explicitly excluded in verse 26. If the dinosaurs are no longer walking the earth (and most scientists say they were extinct) at the time men were finally walking upon the earth, then verse 26 is clear, precise, and without contradiction in this.

Finally, glance ahead at verse 28, where the list of the animals that we shall dominate is repeated. The word translated "moveth," there, is the lighter-on-the-feet, *ramas* again. Considering how much the Hebrews paid particular attention to types of movement, it surely seems the dinosaurs are being pointedly omitted from those things we should have dominion over!

But what are we to make of the passages in Job, which appear to describe two species of dinosaurs and compares their might to the might of men? As I read Job, it only confirms that men would not prevail and have dominion over those beasts. Job doesn't describe any actual confrontation, but only hypothetical encounters, and in neither do men prevail. Job reads as if the author had a vision, or some sort of knowledge of dinosaurs, and was very impressed by them, but was not personally exposed to, or experienced with, dinosaurs.

Whatever we choose to make of Job, it still only shows that men would not have dominated the dinosaurs! It's an interesting matter, to say the least. But it's not the only one raised in this dominion statement.

In Genesis 1:28–29, dominion is reiterated, even to the point of specifying the use of many species for food. Here we find that all the other higher plant and animal species are explicitly covered in terms of our use and dominion. All of the higher species are, but none of the lower ones are! Both the lower plants, such as *deshe,* and the lower animals, such as the *sherets,* are either omitted or ignored. Is this also coincidental, accidental, careless, or is this another pointed exclusion?

The *sherets,* remember, include a lot of life forms, perhaps ranging from insects and other lesser "teeming life" of the swampy waters, all the way down to the bacteria and other such microscopic animals. As we learned in the previous chapter when we were studying verse 20, these insect- and bacteria-types were never explicitly put under the constraint of *miyn,* the genetic "rule of conservation." I suggested the possibility that this lack of *miyn* may explain the apparent rise of ever-newer and ever-more-elusive diseases and insect plagues. I've also suggested that we might want to relate that fact to some of the prophesied horrors in Revelation. So does this omission of dominion here over insects and such animals as viruses and bacteria connect to that? Does it confirm those earlier speculations? It's clearly a possibility, and a very interesting possibility, at that.

As we look at the last few verses of the Creation account, there's little that is directly, or significantly, of concern to our topic and us. Yet there are a few items worth noting, at least to answer some questions some skeptical readers might have. Let's run through them.

> Genesis 1:28 *And God blessed them, and God said unto them, Be fruitful, and multiply, and replenish the earth, and subdue it: and have dominion over the fish of the sea, and over the fowl of the air, and over every living thing that moveth upon the earth.*
> Genesis 1:29 *And God said, Behold, I have given you every herb bearing seed, which is upon the face of all the earth, and every tree, in the which is the fruit of a tree yielding seed; to you it shall be for meat.*
> Genesis 1:30 *And to every beast of the earth, and to every fowl of the air, and to every thing that creepeth upon the earth, wherein there is life, I have given every green herb for meat: and it was so.*

You might wonder whether the "fowl" here is birds or insects. I think birds is most consistent and indicated in the fact that each time it is "fowl of the air (or sky)," and not the *owph* "that may fly over the land."

One of the issues that comes up on occasion is whether there were predators in the Creation account. I've obviously concluded "yes," and interpreted them in the *remes*. If that is so, then one may question whether this assignation of plants as food means that predators were not originally to be meat eaters or scavengers. There is no certain answer, to be sure, in these verses. But note that only *ramas* is used *("to every living thing that creepeth . . . I have given . . . green herb for meat"),* so that leaves the question about *remes* (which I say are the predators) unanswered at the very least. That "herb for meat," by the way, is strictly a King James Version translation; the original word in Hebrew, *oklah,* translated as "meat," is generally translated "food" or "for consuming."

A traditional objection to "predators," of course, comes from a belief that there was no "death" of any sort, not even physical death, on the earth before the Fall, before "sin entered the earth." This is not the place to discuss that major theological premise at length, but it deserves a cursory examination.

WHAT ABOUT MAN? WHAT ABOUT ADAM?

Without death, the earth would have been filled to capacity very quickly. Some might say that's an argument for a "young earth" and the 144-hour Creation. But is it logical? First, just giving one species as food for another entails death for the food. Plants die when we eat them. Individual cells die when we eat only a part of the plant. That would seem to force a retreat to a less absolute statement, or theology, such as "there was no death for animal life." But that leads to the second problem. So many species are superbly "designed" for predation, for scavenging, and for causing decay and transformation of dead plants and animals (and even animal feces!) into "good" stuff, such as compost and fertilizer (in the world we see now), we must wonder where they came from.

If they only exist after the Fall, if they weren't in the original Creation, then when, where, and how did they come to be? Something (surely God) had to have led to, or created quickly, that superbly designed complex, complementary, and efficient plan and scheme of things that we now call the "web of life," the ecology. That ecology, which we see in action today, includes the processes and the processors (animals and plants) that make rich soil and nutrition for plants, which consume and use up the (inevitable?) waste and feces of even "herb eating" animals, as well as the predators that allow the "multiplying" of each species to go on without massive overpopulation. Surely, this system, which not only includes death, but also makes magnificent use of it, had to be designed and created somewhere in our natural history.

It had to be God. He is the only Creator. But, though we are told about the original Creation in Genesis 1, we are not given one word about such a recreation or redesign of the old. If God did "recreate" the plan and redesign, or newly create, a lot of different animals, then at least half of the species alive today, low and high, were recreated or redesigned soon after Genesis 1 or 2. Why are we not told anything about the new creation? Or about the "redesign"? This is a tough bunch of questions, but every answer, except "there were predators in the Creation in Genesis 1," simply creates a lot more questions.

Verse 30 ends with the familiar *hayah,* "it was so" appraisal, and is consistent with the *asah,* which the whole section began with, and not with that one (triple) use of *bara* in verse 27. That also shows that verse 27 was parenthetical (as I said before), a footnote to remind us that Adam, or *ha-adam,* was yet to be created by some very special actions by God. We will learn about them in the next chapter.

Finally, in verse 31, we have the *Elohiym ra-ah kiy towb,* just as we should expect, but with another bit of (very appropriate) expansion. It says, this time, that as He finished all His work (except Adam) as the six-creation days are concluded, God inspected everything that He had *asah,* and that every bit of it was very good, very appropriate, and perfect!

CHAPTER SIX

WHAT ABOUT ADAM? WHAT ABOUT EVE?

Genesis 2 tells the story to which the parenthetical statement in Genesis 1:27 pointed. If you'll recall, we actually paraphrased it as a "new verse" (27a) to help make it very clear just what Genesis 1 had told us. Genesis 1:26 told us that God *asah*-planned to create a mankind (*ha-adam*) in His own image (*tselem*) and likeness (*demuwth*). Verse 27a assures us, parenthetically, that indeed God did exactly that. But the rest of Genesis 1 tells only about His making of *adam* in His own *tselem* and not (yet?) in, or after, His likeness (*demuwth*).

Genesis 1 was only intended to give us a creation account of the natural, physical world in which we live and with which we perceive with our normal senses. After the parentheses of verse 27a, that's all that Genesis 1 does; it finishes that task. Genesis 1 leaves the telling of an *adam* becoming *ha-adam*, of being made into God's *demuwth*, to Genesis 2. We're ready now to begin our probe into that second Creation account. It's almost another book, certainly another story. It's at least as distinct and different from what preceded it (Genesis 1:2 through Genesis 2:3) as was that Creation account of "our world" from the creation of the universe in Genesis 1:1. It has a different focus, perspective, and subject.

When we finish this chapter, we should have a much better understanding of how and why "Man" is not the mere "man" that most scientists and evolutionists would have us believe. I'm sure you know that the questions about "who, what, and why" we are "Mankind," are every bit as important to our children, and our whole society, as all the other "scientific" questions they might ask. Spirit, belief, faith, morality, even self-worth, has evaporated with the modern naturalist/evolutionist definitions of humans as merely marginally more successful animals. The *ha-adam* Man has been reduced, by Evolutionism, back to the mere *adam* man of the natural creation in Genesis 1. I think it is every bit as important we understand the Creation account of Genesis 2 as that of Genesis 1, if we want to avoid the follies of Evolutionary doctrine and benefit most from what science really can offer.

We'll skip the first three verses, Genesis 2:1–3, which only concludes the Creation account of Genesis 1. The next three verses start the new Creation account with a brief recap of the first Genesis 1 and then open the door into the next.

> Genesis 2:4 *These are the generations of the heavens and of the earth when they were created, in the day that the LORD God made the earth and the heavens,*
> Genesis 2:5 *And every plant of the field before it was in the earth, and every herb of the .field before it grew: for the LORD God had not caused it to rain upon the earth, and there was not a man to till the ground*

> Genesis 2:6 *But there went up a mist from the earth, and watered the whole face of the ground.*

Of course, we always miss a few details and shades of meaning if we rely solely on the traditional translations. The ancient scribe's choices of words are never happenstance, but inspired and purposeful, even intended for us of this modern age. We need to always look deeper, but these first three verses are only setting a stage for much to come. I don't want to entangle you in the translating chores here for the small fruit to be gained. Let me simply give you another rendition of the three verses that I think speaks more plainly and more to our own points of interest.

> Genesis 2:4 Those preceding Scriptures are an account of when His heavens and His earth were *bara*-created (from scratch, perhaps *ex nihilo*—the "Big Whoosh"); in the time when the LORD God (*Jehovah Elohiym*) *asah*-created (fashioned, designed *ex materia*) the earth and heavens,
> Genesis 2:5 And before any plant or shrub appeared in His fields in the earth, before any grass or herb grew in His fields. The LORD God had not yet sent any rain to fall upon His earth, and there was not yet any man to till (or make use of) its soils.
> Genesis 2:6 But a mist went up from His earth and watered the whole of them.

There's one especially interesting fact given here, something that ought make one stop and ask, "What's this about?" It's about the rain. We've just read here that there wasn't any rain in the pre-human (pre-*adam*) history.

That's interesting to us for a couple of reasons. The first is that it happens to be that there's a lot of corroborative evidence in the scientific record that the young earth was very warm and very wet, something like a present-day Venus (maybe a bit cooler, though).

So according to both Scripture and science, early Earth was a veritable steaming greenhouse that produced incredibly abundant and, frequently, incredibly large, versions of life—ferns resembling trees, insects as large as eagles, perhaps even reptiles as big as apartment buildings. So is this scriptural detail mere coincidence? I don't think so. To begin with, the Scripture seems to go out of its way to make the point that this greenhouse period was prior to man. It's another great match with the scientific picture of Earth's ancient history. Furthermore, by making an obvious connection to a man (or men, *adam* is not specific) who would come and till, farm, and work the land, the Scripture certainly implies that by the time mankind arrived, the watering system would be different and also implies that part of the work of the future farmer would be utilizing rain (with irrigation?) in farming.

The second point of interest in that detail about mists watering the earth before man was around to till the ground, is what it implies about the lengths of time involved in the Creation account. Somewhere in the details, no matter how we interpret these three verses, whether as referring to a young earth before there was any life, or referring a verdant earth already filled with the higher plants and herbs, there is obviously a span of time when the mists watered the whole face of the earth. There is, in fact, a span of time when the earth and its plants needed watering. It's hardly likely they would have needed watering if we accept that 24-hour Creation-day, 144-hour Creation week interpretation of the Genesis Creation account. God hardly would have needed to tell us He watered His plant kingdom with mists and not rain in a mere forty-eight or seventy-two hour span of time while awaiting the arrival of Adam. So I think we have here, one more reason to argue against the traditional interpretation of *yowm* as twenty-four-hour days and their occurring as six consecutive, sunset-to-sunrise-sunset days, for a total of a 144-hour Creation "week."

It is the next verse, however, which really gets the Genesis 2 narrative started. In verse 7, Man *(ha-adam)* is created.

> Genesis 2:7 *And the LORD God formed man of the dust of the ground, and breathed into his nostrils the breath of life; and man became a living soul.*

This surely must be one of the most significant verses of the Book of Genesis. From out of the first phrase, *"And the LORD God formed man of the dust of the ground"* has come one of the more treasured images of Christians—that of the potter.

The inspiration of that image of God forming a man from a handful of clay, is built mostly upon two words. The first is the "dust," which is found in the traditional translations. But it is the second word that provides the real basis for the image, the Hebrew *yatsar*, which is here translated "formed." *Yatsar* expresses a very strong sense of shaping, fashioning, and designing, and the Hebrews commonly did use it to denote the potter's labor. I think one reason they used it so is that *yatsar* also carries that additional sense of "for a higher purpose," or of "creating something now to meet a future plan or purpose," which we found in the verb *yatsa* (many authorities think it's the same word). That added connotation no doubt makes *yatsar* all the more appropriate for the potter's work.

Think about it. The immediate and obvious task of making a clay pot is probably the least part of the tradesman's task. More importantly, every pot must be carefully fashioned and formed for a purpose, for its own particular intended use. Its specific future use must always inform and guide the *yatsar* act. The pot remains a useless object until it's placed in the hands of the one whom it will serve and until it is fulfilling the purpose for which it was designed and made. In that way, *yatsar* simply does not comprehend forming "a useless object," something without purpose. And just as a pot is a vessel that must be carefully fashioned to hold that which it will and serve as it should, so Christians have taken from this verse 7 that same understanding that man was created as a vessel to receive and hold something and serve some special purposes. We must admit that it's a powerful symbolism and expressive image which *yatsar* and "dust" evoke. It's one I've long enjoyed and used myself.

But, as usual, there is another way we can interpret the original language that meets a different use—an interpretation that meets and resolves some serious scientific conflicts and questions. We can start working out our alternative interpretation by first looking at a portion of verse 2:19:

> *And out of the ground the LORD God formed every beast of the field, and every fowl of the air . . .*

This is the same verb, *yatsar,* now being used in connection with all the higher animal species. The connotations are the very same as we saw in *yatsa,* when used in Genesis 1:24, where God said the *erets* (earth, or the land) should "produce" the higher species. Thus verses 1:24, 2:7, and 2:19 all use the same, or essentially the same, verb, *yatsa(r).* There is no apparent contradiction or variance there, only perfect consistency. Hold on to that thought.

Now what about this "dust"? The "dust" of verse 2:7 comes from *aphar,* which is often representing something dry and crumbly, but not necessarily "clay." In fact, *aphar* has, as do so many of the ancient Hebrew lexicon, quite a wide set of referents. It can be used to signify "dust," "powder," "ashes," even "rubbish and debris." But there is one even more interesting, I think. *Aphar* can also mean "ore," as of the minerals of the earth. In fact, *aphar* is the only word one can find in the ancient lexicon for "ores" or "minerals," while numerous other Hebrew words are used for, and considered more appropriate, for both "dust" and "clay." And one more point: The dust is of the "ground." But in verse 1:24, the word *erets* is used, which is basically referring more to the "land" than the ground, as in soil and dirt. Here, in Genesis 2:7, the word is *adamah,* which almost always points to the soil. In fact, some say the word *adam* comes from *adamah,* making a connection between the common color of the soil, and man. At any rate, what we see is that the *adamah* from which the man was *yatsar*-fashioned is much more "soil" and "dirt" than is *erets.*

So here's where we're going with this: Translating *aphar* as "ores" or "minerals" leads us to a useful bit of recently acquired science knowledge. Verse 2:7 becomes a statement that can even be seen as another signpost. Only in modern times has science and chemical analysis shown us that our bodies are truly composed of the minerals of the earth. In fact, medical science is still discovering just how much we require the *aphar* of *adamah* in our nutrition for continued good health, and how we must eat a balanced diet of the plants and animals we are commanded to eat in order to get them. So with *aphar* rendered "minerals" or "ores," that first part of verse 7, may also be read as, "And the LORD God formed men out of the minerals of the earth . . ."

So far, we are still dealing primarily with the "physical" creation, even in regards to man. But the shift begins in this first phrase in Genesis 2:7, as the Man is now *ha-adam.* Most of what we deal with concerns those aspects of man, the human species (mere *adam*), that set it apart and make it something more than any other species; things that make it Man (*ha-adam*), a species touched by, or in relationship with God. But before we go further, let's review what we have learned, so far, that is peculiar to the creation of man.

First, we read in Genesis 1:27 that man was *bara*-created. We know from our study of the precise meanings of Hebrew vocabulary that *bara* is the most "absolute sense of creation," and that it is creation by God Himself, not by another agent or agency (like earth, water, or even, by implication, a natural law). *Bara* is always a new sort of creation: In Genesis 1:1 it is the "Big Whoosh;" in Genesis 1:21 it is about the dinosaurs; in Exodus it is creating brand new marvels; in Numbers 16:30 it is creating "a new thing." But since we see in Genesis 2:19 and in Genesis 1:24 that the other higher animals were also made of the dust or minerals of the earth, we can probably conclude *"yatsar* of *aphar"* is not part of the *bara* aspect of man.

Second, we read in Genesis 1:26 that man was *asah* (created), designed to be in God's own *tselem* (image).

Third, we read also that man was intended to be *demuwth* (like) Him, to share in some sort of mind, soul, or spirit qualities of God that go beyond just image or form.

Fourth, we read also in Genesis 1:26 that man was set into a special ecological "niche" (that is scientific for "relationship," the way a species adapts to and utilizes the whole of its environment). Mankind is to "have complete dominion"(1:26); and in 2:5 we are clued into the fact that men, or a man, will be also expected, or appointed, to "husband" and "till" the land, which is also a kind of dominion which extends to the plants and the ground.

Now, as we continue with the next part of verse 7, we read, *"and breathed into his nostrils the breath of life."* This appears to be something very direct and unique, no other kind or species is touched or treated this way. At this moment, the man is already physically created; he has already, at the minimum, a physical body. Is it that he just needed "breath," to have his lungs filled with air, or the *chay*-life sort of vitality put into him by the Creator? I don't think so. All the other creatures came complete with such life and vitality. So I don't think he needed any extra "kick start" just to be alive. So what about this "breath of life"? Just what is it, and is it the source of whatever it is that sets this one creature apart and makes him something that God should *bara*-create him? Well, let's see if there's any more to learn from the original language.

That phrase which is rendered, "and breathed into his nostrils the breath of life," comes from four words in the Hebrew vocabulary, which we read as "breathed," "nostrils," "breath," and "life." Here is the fuller range of appropriate meanings of each:

NAPHACH: blow, puff, expire, kindle

APH: nostril, face, person

NESHAMAH: breath, breath of God or man or animal, wind, spirit, divine wisdom

CHAY: life(!), soul (appetites, will, and mind, not necessarily wisdom), animal vitality.

As always, there are many ways we can read or envision that brief bit of Scripture. We could understand it pretty simply, even mundanely, as "God blew the first breath into the lungs of the new (infant?) man." Or, we could interpret it something like this: "God clasped the face of the man between His hands and inspired, into His chosen one, a portion of His *neshamah*. *Neshamah* certainly looks like a good candidate for supplying the mysterious, defining essence of what is unique, or God-created-special, in Man, but is it? Should we now assume that that is what is being confirmed in the remainder of verse 7, *"and man became a living soul"*? We need to consider a few more things about the whole verse.

The first thing that caught my attention when I delved into the original Hebrew was that starting here, we have the *ha-adam* Man. That is not just a man, but a Man that became a living soul. In verse 2:5, we still had *adam* man. As I've said, from this point on, it never changes. It will always be *ha-adam,* to be translated as "Adam," or "Man," rather than "man." I would almost interpret it as "His chosen man."

That led me to look more closely at the "living soul." Is this "living soul" something special or unique, which no other creatures have? The answer, which surprised me, is no. The source word, *nephesh,* has nothing special about it, nothing that would seem unique to Man, in all of its collection of meanings. Everything it connotes is pretty much equally applied to any (but especially, higher) living animal. Indeed, *nephesh* appears in Genesis 1:20, 1:21, and 1:24, where it is always translated as "creature," and only indicates exactly "a living creature." Even when used later in Scripture, in narrations about people and history, it still only refers to the physical life of persons. Whatever *nephesh* is, it is shared by both the lower and higher forms of animal life and is not unique to Man. For example, we find it in Genesis 1:30, where God declares, "to every *(chay)* living animal, beast and fowl, to which I have given *(chay nephesh)* life, I give leaf and grass for food" (my paraphrase).

But if we look at *nephesh* as it is being used in Genesis 9, we may have found something to help explain just what it is. In Genesis 9:4, God tells Noah that he and his descendants may eat animal flesh, but He forbids eating it as long as the "life" *(nephesh)*, which is "the blood" *(dam)*, is still in it. A few verses later He makes His covenant—promising no more floods—with every *(nephesh)* creature, not just mankind. It certainly appears, from this, that *nephesh* itself is something shared and equivalent between animals and men and is not supplying any special defining difference between animals and us.

But here's a rather intriguing point. While forbidding the taking of animal life with its *nephesh* and *dam,* in verse 9:4, God declares no penalty. In the next verse, Genesis 9:5, He also forbids the taking of life of *ha-adam* (His human), and for the killing of this *ha-adam,* there is a death penalty—for any Man or beast—who violates His injunction.

The next verse, Genesis 9:6, provides another surprise, a real surprise. The injunction against killing of any *ha-adam* is restated, but this is an express injunction against any *adam!* The Scripture appears to be addressing two distinct types of creatures, *adams* and *ha-adams!* Furthermore, the Scripture not only forbids any man from killing any Man, it explains the injunction with this rationale: "For the *(ha-adam)* Man has been made in the *(tselem)* image of God" (my paraphrase). Now that has to give us pause to think. Apparently *nephesh* is important, but not enough to define *ha-adam*. *Tselem,* is obviously important also, but is it enough? *Tselem,* you recall, was mentioned in Genesis 1:27, but is not mentioned again until Genesis 9:6. Not only that, elsewhere in the Scriptures it is frequently used in regard to idols and other images. So *tselem* alone, I think, is also not enough, not capable of separately accounting for what *ha-adam* Man is.

All of this convinces me that we have to go further, looking beyond any single element or quality to understand the uniqueness and special place of Man in the Creation. If one word should be a candidate, it is *demuwth*. But so far, the evidence is not in, and I'm afraid we need to continue to build the list we've already begun. Perhaps when we are done, we will find what we are looking for.

The next verse, Genesis 2:8, tells us what the Lord God did with the Man He had just made, or selected and transformed.

Genesis 2:8 And the LORD God planted a garden eastward in Eden; and there he put the man whom he had formed.

God had already "planted" the whole earth in Genesis 1. It was reaffirmed that He had in verses 2:4–6. Now, in verse 8, we are told that He set apart a special portion of "His fields." The King James Version, it is true, says God "planted" this "garden," but the Hebrew word *nata* does not necessarily mean plant. It also means "establish" or "fix." And the Hebrew word *gan*, translated "garden," literally denotes an "enclosure." And there is another interesting alternative translation that can be made of the word we read as "eastward" in our King James. The Hebrew is *qedem*; it also translates as "of old" or "from the earliest times."

"Eastward" means very little to us today. No one has any idea where the Garden of Eden might have been. There is no evidence that even Moses had any idea where it was or where eastward of the Garden would be. But the suggestion that there was a place—already established, set up, and set apart from the very beginning in the "earliest of times;" and that this separate and enclosed place (a "paradise") was intended for the Man He planned to create—is an idea that certainly makes great sense, fits well with what we know of the ways and personality of God, and fits very much with the original Hebrew language. This is then another good rendering of verse 8:

> Genesis 2:8 The LORD God had established a place in Eden, from the earliest of times, and there He put the Man which He created *(yatsar)*.

It's not a great difference in translation, but it reads more sensibly as I see it, and increases our sense of God's developing of a plan and program in all the Creation. *Yatsar* says He had further purposes for the Man; this garden was a place, set apart from very early on, long before the Man even existed; and it points to some more new ideas we're about to uncover.

I think the new interpretation of verse 8 helps us understand two trees we read about in verse 9. Genesis 2:9 tells us that within that place, the enclosure where God placed His Man, were two of the most powerful manifestations of the supernatural on earth: the tree of life, whose fruit bestowed unending life, and the tree of knowledge of good and evil, in which resided the potential for "not God," or for plainly choosing to not believe or obey God. In the midst of this very special place, prepared very early in the scheme of Creation, were both the essence of the heart of God, and the heart of Lucifer. More than trees, they were powers—no matter how they were manifested materially. It seems very unlikely to me that God would have carried them there after the Man was created, but more likely that they were already there when the Man was brought from the "earliest of times."

WHAT ABOUT ADAM? WHAT ABOUT EVE?

Is this an issue of theology or science? Well, you cannot separate science and theology easily. Many scientists today may profess a "theology-neutrality," but the founding fathers of science were not neutral, and most philosophers of science (prior to this decade) have never thought science is theology-neutral. Certainly, if you observe the increasingly shrill debate between Evolutionists and Creationists, there is no theological neutrality. In fact, modern science has largely become a religion itself, a faith or belief of not-God. I know. I was raised a scientist, and as I was trained, we still had to study the philosophy (theology and doctrine) of science right along with everything else.

It's in the Garden that the two predominant theologies of your and my world meet head on. The first "tree," the "tree of life," is a window unto the very same power that we believe created everything, starting with that initial moment the scientists call a "Big Bang." We generally believe, also, that what that power can create, that same power can renew and sustain. That concept is exactly what the Scriptures are telling us about here in the "tree of life."

Atheists, and almost every modern scientist, think the tree in the garden is foolishness, simply literary nonsense. They don't believe in an actual locus of a power of eternal creativity, let alone try to picture one, except perhaps in the locus of the power of their "Big Bang." But is not our tree, with its power of eternal life, nothing more than just the opposite of another ongoing "impossible" reality (which most scientists do choose to believe in), the ultimate fount of "absolute destruction," the "black hole"? Indeed, most scientists do believe in "black holes." They now believe, in fact, that there are many of them, both far and near. Is a tree of eternal life and creativity not every bit as likely as a hole of eternal death and destruction? Perhaps "black holes" are but doorways into perdition!

The second tree, as any psychologist or sociologist or theologian should guess, hardly needed to be a tree. That the Creator chose such a form is merely His choice. But it really needed be nothing more than an opportunity of any shape or form—an opportunity to make a clear choice, to choose "not God," to choose disobedience. It could have been a blackboard where the Man could write out his choice, just as easily as a tree with forbidden fruit. The "serpent" could have told him how to write his disobedience just as easily.

In a very real sense, that's what we are dealing with, today. Even if your child were raised in a perfect Christian family and community, schooled only in Christian schools, and never taught how to choose not-God, there will be a place and a time when he or she will have the chance to learn how to choose not-God, and write it on his or her "blackboard." Man, the Scripture tells us, was designed with free will and choice. So it's God's purpose and will that we each have the choice and the opportunity to exercise it. Even Lucifer and all the angels had that same opportunity!

What about the actual reality of the two trees? Of course, skeptics will point to them as proof of the "fictional" nature of the Bible. Well, anyone who takes that position and yet accepts wholeheartedly the latest in scientific notions like singularities, "Big Bang," and black holes, is being wholly inconsistent, or is very ignorant. All such things like singularities, "Big Bangs," and black holes, are thoroughly figurative, literary constructs, written in a language and imagery by scientists and mathematicians alike. They are still nothing but inventive literary constructs about unknowable things or data. They are all things that no one has ever actually seen or touched! The words are convenient inventions standing in as pro-tem descriptions for some unexplainable things that seem to be going on in the so-called "natural world." I repeat, none of the above three examples have ever been seen. In fact, they are things that no one can ever see by definition! It takes faith and commitment to believe in them. We all simply have to decide which book to believe: the one written four years ago, or the one written four thousand years ago. The real test should be which one explains the most. So, read on!

Our Genesis 2 Creation account gets back on to a more mundane (natural) track in verse 15. There, though rather indirectly, we will find some more clues about the nature, history, and meaning of Man.

> Genesis 2:15 *And the LORD God took the man, and put him into the garden of Eden to dress it and to keep it.*

Each of the four verbs here are translated in the King James in such a way as to create a picture of a childlike or simple young man being physically picked up and set in place to work. I imagine that you, like I, more or less picture this place like some royal English garden, such as Buckingham Palace. Yet each of the verbs in the verse are more commonly used in very different ways and carry implications that paint a rather different picture. A picture that fits together better and better as we go.

The word translated "took" is the Hebrew *laqach*. That is the same word that was commonly used for "taking" a bride, and it normally conveys more the idea of "chose" or "led."

The word translated "put" is *yanach* and is probably better understood as "settled him," as in "gave him a place to live."

The word translated "to dress" is *abad*. Rather than "dressing" the garden, *abad* should better be read as "to labor" in it, or to "till the land," generally as a servant. You could interpret it as "he was put in the garden to serve God." There is nothing in the word actually that suggests, "dressing" plants in a garden. Nor is it obvious why God would need such labor. If we look elsewhere in the Scriptures, we find it is the same word that is used for the seven years that Jacob labored for Laban in order to gain his daughter in marriage. It was used for Moses' serving God during the Exodus, and it was used to describe the Levites' role in the temple.

Finally, the word translated "to keep" is *shamar*. To *shamar* the garden, means to "guard," "protect," and "honor and preserve" it. You shouldn't think it conveys any idea of planting flowers or sweeping paths. Cain, in fact, impudently asked God, using this *shamar,* "Am I my brother's keeper?" And God commanded the Israelites to so "keep" (guard and preserve) His commandments and His festivals.

The benefit of all this re-translating, I think, is that it shows us Adam was neither a child nor a simple gardener. This Adam was quite adult and given adult responsibilities. In fact, he looks more like a partner in the farm. This Man was given dominion (he ruled the farm), the duty to respect and protect the farm (like the head servant of several parables), and was charged with attending this Garden much as a priest attends a temple. This Adam certainly reminds one of a Levite priest, or an Abraham, who was "chosen" and placed in a covenant relationship with God. Perhaps he was the very first chosen one; chosen in a way similar to the way that Moses, Aaron, or Abram, were all chosen later.

After a while—how long we don't know—God makes a decision.

> Genesis 2:18 *And the LORD God said, It is not good that the man should be alone; I will make him an help meet for him.*

We know that Adam had already spent quite a long time in the garden; it could have been centuries according to the life spans of others, even after the "Fall." At any rate, God declares that it was "not a good, kind, beneficial, or right-for-the-plan, situation." Remember *towb?* That was the word used in God evaluating the results of a *yowm's* creations. That's the word used here. It "is not good the Man should be (or have become, it's from *hayah!*) alone." That "alone" is also an interesting term. It comes from *bad,* which means more than just being "single" alone, or "only" alone. It generally means alone by being "separated," "apart," "by itself." That, with *hayah*, very strongly implies this *ha-adam* was not always alone, but had become separated and alone.

When God says, "I will make (*asah*-fashion, prepare, appoint) a companion (a mate that succors or helps, in the sense of delivers or protects!) for him," there are a lot of implications in the Hebrew that are ignored or lost in our traditional interpretations.

First, there is the strong implication, which we just brought out, that the Man was not created as a single, lone creature, but was alone by dint of a separation, which was further strengthened by the *hayah*—"it came to be" alone.

Second, we traditionally assume the answer God intended to use to solve Adam's loneliness was "another little helper," such as "a little woman to do some chores for him" (well, maybe an assistant gardener). The actual Hebrew uses a word, *ezer*, which, when used elsewhere, refers to more help than you and I might imagine. *Ezer* is help such as the might of King David would provide his friends and even refers to the protection and deliverance, which the Lord Himself provides. There is a feminine side of *ezer*, involving a sort of motherly "succoring" or "nursing." But if you read the Scriptures on mothers' roles and the power of the womb, you'll realize "mother," in the Bible, is a power-full concept, more like "mother grizzly!"

It looks to me like the picture drawn here in 2:18 by the Hebrew language is that the Man was growing up and was not without emotional and sexual needs, to the point it was getting very serious, or morally dangerous. The Man needed to be protected (*ezer*) against something. Yet that begs a question: If he was the first, the one and only, with not even a female created yet, where did such problems come from? There are no other females he could get into trouble with, and if he were a complete neophyte, he wouldn't even know how.

There's a third problem in our linguistics. Two Hebrew words were kind of jury-rigged together to come up with what the King James Version translated "help meet." The first was the word we just discussed, *ezer*. The second, *neged*, is generally translated "conspicuously," "in the sight of," or in the presence of." More than just "for him," this word suggests "with him," or "right there with him." Now here's what I'm really thinking about in this: If you had a son who was beginning to look at the girls on the street corner (in inappropriate ways), you might say, "I better get this kid married!" To do that in historical Jewish culture, you would bring in an appropriate (Jewish, spiritually-right) girl, and you'd arrange a betrothal. That's exactly what the language implies God was thinking.

But what is it the Lord does? Look at the next two verses:

> Genesis 2:19 *And out of the ground the LORD God formed every beast of the field, and every fowl of the air; and brought them unto Adam to see what he would call them: and whatsoever Adam called every living creature, that was the name thereof.*
> Genesis 2:20 *And Adam gave names to all cattle, and to the fowl of the air, and to every beast of the field, but for Adam there was not found an help meet for him.*

That's a surprise, isn't it? After deciding things are getting really serious and the Man needs a "girlfriend," the first thing God does is start parading each and every higher animal kind that He'd created past him, just "to see what he would call them." Talk about a non-sequitur!

(Some think verse 19 is announcing a new set of creation. It is not. It is a parenthetical statement, making it perfectly clear that (1) God created all these creatures, and (2) He brings only the higher level beasts and birds past the Man, whom we'll usually call Adam from now on.)

But, really, we know the "name game" was not the sole purpose of the parade and that it was seriously related to the search for his new "friend." We are expressly told that by way of verse 20: "but there was not a help meet found for him." So obviously, the parade of species was at least partly intended to enable a search for that "help meet."

Can we assume God wanted to see if Adam would choose a "help meet"—let's say, "mate"—from amongst the animals? Seems impossible, doesn't it? Surely God didn't actually expect some lion, giraffe, or whatever, would qualify. Did God just want to see if Adam was dumb enough, confused enough, or becoming depraved enough, to go for one of them? Hardly likely. Perhaps there were some "closer calls" in the parade, some creatures such as apes or chimpanzees that Adam might go for? A little more likely. Would God have allowed him to choose one of them? Hardly likely. What if there were some really close calls in the parade? What if there were some other hominids—some almost-man-types, such as Neanderthals or other hominid species—some almost-*Homo sapiens* in the lineup? Now that could be a serious possibility, if we believe scientists really have unearthed scores of fossils of early almost-men. It would make more sense of the parade.

In fact, there might have been an even a greater test for Adam, something of real significance. Suppose Adam had to learn or demonstrate that he had developed some true spiritual "discernment." Suppose Adam was even going to see a female as "modern" as himself, as *Homo sapien* as himself, but lacking something of discernable importance, such as that "breath of spirit," or whatever he received when God chose and then "fashioned" him from amongst a sea of "mere men." Could we read these Scriptures as telling us Adam had actually been chosen in much the same Abram was chosen from amongst all the men of his time? Had Adam been chosen, sanctified by covenant, and set apart into Eden, separated from the rest of the men and women of his time? Was that why the Garden had been prepared in the earliest of times?

Are there any answers to these questions? Perhaps. They are all, at least, reasonable and legitimate questions; indeed, almost inevitable questions, if we pay serious attention to the Genesis text. They're practically built-in, I think, for any late twentieth-century reader, whether a believer or not. And the fact that they are so apparent, and so obvious, to the astute reader of our time, leads me to suspect that once again we are being given in these details about Adam, another signpost. Very few people have ever suspected Genesis had anything to say about prehistoric hominids (species much like ours) or other men living at the time of Adam. Indeed, no one—3500 years ago—had any idea that such creatures existed. So much of what we have just covered, not in the least the original language about *adam*-men and *ha-adam*-Men, has to raise new interest in open-minded people about the authenticity and veracity of the Genesis Creation account. And there is more to come!

Everything in the Creation account that we've read to this point has been very reasonable in terms of everyday knowledge and thinking. Though some folks may not want to believe God is the creation force, open minds should admit it's a reasonable hypothesis, especially in light of the details we've uncovered about the Creation outline and the signposts pointing the way to what we now know 3500 years later. And nothing in the account contradicts logic or the principles of physics we are finally coming to know, nor the practical biological and physical observations our researches have provided. But the next two verses in Genesis 2 are an exception.

The story of the "rib" taken from Adam and this exceptional and uncharacteristic method of creating the woman, Eve, is difficult to understand. It seems pretty inconsistent with the rest of the Creation account. It may contradict Genesis 1:27, and it is one element that will not reconcile with even the simplest scientific knowledge, such as the fact men and women have the same number of ribs. It's always been a part of the Bible I've always had to just "put on the shelf," and ignore. But once I began to work on this book, I found myself constantly returning to pick it up and take another look.

When the answer to my questions finally began to emerge, I strongly resisted it myself. I felt the rib story was just too much of a sacred cow in Christian circles. Everyone knows the story of Eve; it's practically a video clip in most of our minds, a staple of Sunday school and sermons. So however inconsistent with the rest of the Creation account and with our sure knowledge of physiology, however much it challenges us in science class and raises jokes among the unbelievers, I still hesitated to tamper with it. But the new interpretation that came out of the Hebrew (almost against my wishes) finally won out. And now, as I read it, I've become very pleased and happy about it. It restores the consistency of the flow and process of the Creation account, and I think it reveals to us why God has so continually been very adamant in His concern with our sexual mores and marriage (marriage is, to the anthropologist, a defining characteristic of *ha-adam* human life).

Let's take another good look at God's answer to Adam's need of a mate.

> Genesis 2:21 *And the LORD God caused a deep sleep upon Adam, and he slept: and he took one of his ribs, and closed up the flesh instead thereof;*
> Genesis 2:22 *And the rib, which the LORD God had taken from man, made he a woman, and brought her unto the man.*

As always, we find here that there are quite a number of possible meanings for every original Hebrew word. What we learn, in this case, as we sort out all the words of these two verses, is that each and every one of the original words is compatible with two distinct and separate lines of interpretation. They can all line up

"Hey Mom, What About Dinosaurs?"

into two different, but consistent, sets of meaning, so they can tell two very different stories. And to tell the truth, the new alternative interpretation, which I will present here, actually hangs together better than the traditional rib-into-woman account. It both integrates a couple of awkward moments in the traditional version (i.e. "instead thereof," in verse 21; and keeping to the original word order of verse 22, while the traditional does not), and holds truer to traditional Hebraic uses of all the original Hebrew language.

As usual, it helps us to look at the create-verb first. The Scripture says, a bit awkwardly, that God "made . . . a woman." "Made," it turns out, did not come from any of the previously used create-verbs, but came from *banah*. *Banah* is not really a "creation" word at all. It requires a real stretch to convey that meaning. Instead, it means "establish" or "build," as in "build a family," not as in "build a boat or a body!" It is also commonly used to stand for the "making a mother" out of a woman by any of several means. These means could include giving her children by her use as a concubine (were she only barren) and the common Hebrew practice of the levirate, where a widow marries or lies with her deceased husband's brother. This true meaning of *banah*, we shall see, becomes an extraordinarily appropriate and convincing correction and strongly supports my alternative to the King James Version's interpretation.

Having first looked at the create-verb, let's walk through the rest of the two verses carefully, almost word by word. Verse 21 first:

> *And the Lord God caused a deep sleep upon Adam, and he slept: and he took one of his ribs, and closed up the flesh instead thereof.*

It begins with ". . . *the LORD God caused a deep sleep (trance) to fall upon Adam. . . .*" That much is OK the way it is translated. After that, however, the alternative meanings to each word become nificant, consistent, and cumulative:

"and He took": "Took" comes from *laqach*, which is generally translated as "took a wife" or "brought to marry," as well as, "procured," "fetched," "chose," "captured," or "selected." All are for the express purpose of betrothal and marriage. In fact, the few times *laqach* is not used for taking wives, it is used for "taking in, into, or unto oneself." It is never translated "out of" or "away from" something. That is, it is a flat contradiction to use that verb to take a "thing" out of Adam.

"one": "One" comes from *echad*, which is frequently used to indicate one, but it also means "a certain" or "certain one." Together, in the most common usage, the two words would most probably be read as, "He brought a certain one (for marriage)."

"his ribs": "The rib" is at the heart of the matter here. Let's bypass it, for a moment, while we work through the rest of the passage and come to thoroughly understand the context around that rib, then we can best judge our re-translation of the rib.

"and closed up": "Closed up" is translated from *cagar* (pronounced "sawgar"). That is a very unusual interpretation of *cagar*. Ordinarily the word means to "enclose" or "shut in," as in "close the door on"; it serves as "quarantine" in the Levitical rules for health. Otherwise, *cagar* normally translates as "surrender," "deliver," or "give over."

"the flesh": "Flesh" comes from *basar*. *Basar* is indeed flesh, but it is also the more base, worldly sense of flesh, as in carnal. It was often used as a euphemism ("polite" substitution) for male sexual organs. Interestingly, the root of this word is one that speaks of "good news," or "gladden."

"instead thereof": Here is a phrase that never made sense to me. I just assumed it made sense in 1611. Nowadays, translators tend to render it something like "in the place" (i.e. place of the wound left from taking out a rib), which certainly fits better with the rest of the translated text. But, as always, we need see what are we translating from in the Hebrew text. The word is *tachath*. *Tachath* has several different uses. It usually means "for the sake of" or "for a definite purpose." If it should ever translate as "in the place," then it is "in the place of," as in "substitution." It is also used for the position "under." Even that translation, "under," you'll see, supports our objection to the old translation and supports our substitution. The form of *tachath* used here in verse 21 is actually a rare form of the word. If we search throughout the Scriptures for a close parallel, the best match comes in 2 Samuel 22:40 and 22:48, where it expresses a special sense of "under;" that of "subjection" or "conquest." Other places similar usages refer to a woman "conquered" by a man. Are we beginning to get a rather spicy, R-rated picture?

OK. Now verse 22:

And the rib, which the LORD God had taken from man, made he a woman, and brought her unto the man.

We start out with the rib again, but let's continue to wait on that one. Let's let the context build up our case.

"which": "Which" comes from a rather vague, relative pronoun *aher.* It can also translate as a "who" or a "that." It doesn't discriminate gender or number.

"had taken": "Taken" is from that same *laqach* as in verse 21, meaning "procured" or "brought for marriage."

"from": "From" is from *min,* which may also translate as "from out of" in the sense of "separating from."

"man": "Man" is from *adam,* which you'll remember is a very inclusive word, referring to a man, many men, all men, all mankind, a person, and human beings.

" made": "Made" is from *banah* again and is still a very unlikely translation. *Banah* best translates "establish or set up," as of, a family. But in this case, there's another problem with the translation. The word appears to us completely out of place. *Banah* starts the verse in the original Hebrew! It doesn't attach to the woman! She belongs to the second verb, *laqach*, which means "brought for betrothal"! Confusing? Well, apparently the translators reversed the placement of the two verbs because it worked better to keep the sense of the "story" they thought was being told. As you'll see, we won't need to do that in our interpretation.

So far, we've worked through all of *"And the rib, which the LORD God had taken from man, made He . . ."* The rest of the verse reads, *". . . a woman and brought her unto the man . . ."*

"woman": "Woman" comes from the word *ishshah*, which also means "wife."

"brought": "Brought" is the verb *bow* in the original Hebrew Scripture. The King James Version translates it as "and brought" her. That, however, neglects a major aspect of the Hebrew word. Remember how much the ancient Hebrews are concerned with motion, how they really detail everything about motions? Well, usually, *bow* strongly indicates "to go in" or "enter," as into a room or situation. That's not made clear in the King James Version's simple "brought." It would be better indicated by saying this woman was "brought into," "lead into," or even, "entered" the place where Adam slept.

"OK," you say, "it says, 'brought unto the man.' Doesn't that cover it?" No, not quite. Why? Because there was a second word in the Hebrew, *el*, which is credited for the "unto." Apparently the King James Version ignored the "into" because of the explicit "unto." What's the difference? If the "unto" or "into" was already provided by the verb, the *el* should have contributed a stronger idea of "toward" or "unto," even, denoting "for a purpose." The following is a better sense of what was originally written: "The woman was brought in, ushered in unto Adam (for some purpose)."

All these details paint an ever-stronger "bedroom" or "bridal chamber" and "first night" kind of picture. But where is the bedroom, the nuptial chamber? Well, that is what the "rib" is! The Hebrew word, translated as a rib, is *tsela*. *Tsela* has several uses. In none of them, outside of this single instance, is it considered a human rib. The only time, in all the Bible, that *tsela* is translated as a human rib is in this story! Usually the word refers to the side, or edge of something; sometimes to planks or curved boards, as would be found in the ribbing of a boat. But *tsela* is also used on many occasions, to refer to rooms or chambers. This occurs, usually, when the rooms are around the outside (thus the "side" aspect of the word) of a house or building.

Now, here's a helpful lesson about basic words in the Hebrew language. Their words, as we understand them, like *tsela*, are constantly modified with additions to their basic structure, or spelling. The speaker adds prefixes and suffixes and makes internal changes to reflect grammar and syntax and to create multiple-word meanings. For example, *tsela* in 1King 6:5 has been modified to *yaatsiya*! Yet it still means "chamber." But if we look in Ezekiel 41, where the prophet was taken by God into a vision to see the future temple (see 41:9, for the best example) we can see the word in its most exact repeat of the form used in Genesis 2:21 and 22. There, in Ezekiel, *tsela* is definitely about "rooms." In fact, in Ezekiel, the *tsela* are sleeping chambers in the temple! So there we have it. We have the perfect linguistic match, and our "rib" is definitely a "sleeping chamber." It provides an extraordinary piece of evidence (which I had verified by my independent expert in Hebrew) supporting our alternative translation of Genesis 2:21–22.

This, I believe, is a very reasonable and consistent translation of the original Hebrew Scripture:

> Genesis 2:21 The Lord God caused a trance to come over Adam, and He brought to the chamber where he slept, a chosen female, and delivered her for the purposes of the flesh.
> Genesis 2:22 The Lord God established the family in that chamber, where He brought for marriage a woman from among men, and ushered her in unto Adam.

That's quite a different story, isn't it? Instead of a strange and extraordinary act, and an exception to the pattern of the rest of Creation, it tells of a rather normative act, however significant, and implies it was similar to the special creation that made Adam. We don't have to try to imagine something strange or try to reconcile it with plain biology by our own additional hypotheses. There's nothing here beyond explanation in terms and processes already part of the Creation account. As it reads here, this story comfortably reminds us of the covenant-making with Abram. And, it does one more remarkable thing: It brings marriage and family up to the level of a creation act by God and shows those uniquely human institutions as part of the very creation plan of God. They've been long recognized by anthropologists as a major part of whatever it is that makes us human. And they've always been something that God zealously demands we honor and respect and maintain from beginning of the Scriptures!

If the Scripture is the truth, and our translating of these Scriptures is true, then there should be confirmation in both other Scripture and the natural world. We can plainly see that this re-translation better fits the observable natural world. We can also see that it is consistent, at least, with the Scriptures that have preceded it, and some we've referred to that follow it. Consistency is, to be sure, the essence of both good scientific technique and biblical scholarship. Equally important, in science and normative scholarship, is predictive consistency. What that means for us is that if our new version is accurate, it will not be contradicted by, and may even improve the consistency and our understanding of, subsequent Scriptures.

We haven't got much left to go in the Creation record to give us any opportunity for predictive testing and confirmation, but there are several worthwhile opportunities. We can start with the very next verse, Genesis 2:23. For this, and verse 24, I want to also give you two more modern and popular translations, The Revised Standard Version and The Living Bible, along with our usual King James Version.

> Genesis 2:23 *And Adam said, This is now bone of my bones, and flesh of my flesh: she shall be called Woman, because she was taken out of man.* (KJV)

> Genesis 2:23 *Then the man said, "This at last is bone of my bones and flesh of my flesh; she shall be called Woman, because she was taken out of man."* (RSV)

> Genesis 2:23 *"This is it!" Adam exclaimed. "She is part of my own bone and flesh! Her name is 'woman' because she was taken out of a man."* (TLB)

We probably all agree that the essence of what Adam is saying, is "Now this person is one like me!" If we had just read the traditional "rib story" and accepted it as factual, we'd probably also conclude that Adam is saying it because he knows "she was made from meat and bone of my own body." Apparently he's not even shocked or surprised! The King James Version's "This is now . . ." even sounds like he's rather matter of fact about it. The "at last" of the Revised Standard Version on the other hand, is a bit more curious interpretation. It's as if he was saying, "What took you so long to do this (strange) thing?" And The Living Bible gives us yet another somewhat intriguing impression: It's as if Adam is saying, "Now you've got it right!"

One wonders how they could all come up with such different pictures of that moment. Perhaps it's because they are trying to make sense out of a rather difficult-to-picture event. The Hebrew language, by the way, could also be interpreted in a much more likely "Look. This one is finally . . .," as if he's showing her to the Lord God and telling Him the long search is over; that "this one fits the bill!" This is interesting, but it's not the crux of the problem.

I think we're missing more than just some details or some sense of Adam's little speech; we are actually missing a very profound observation that Adam is expressing. We can miss it for two reasons. First, the "rib" interpretation predisposes us as much as it did the translators, to assume he's referring to the meat and bone of the rib. One might wonder how he could have known about it, having been unconscious, but that's a minor curiosity, readily explained by an assumption or two. From our own re-translation, however, we can take it as a certainty that he is not actually equating her with any actual bone or meat of his own. Yet we can still fail to understand his real meaning in "bone of my bone, flesh of my flesh" because we don't understand what the meaning of that phrase, especially the "bone of my bone," is to an ancient Hebrew.

Most of us nowadays think of bones strictly as mere bones, pretty much as the dead and lifeless leftovers of a material, mechanical body. The Hebrews, in contrast, saw in the bones the essence, essentially the spiritual essence, of the person who once resided in, or was wrapped around those bones. They understood a lot more by the remains in those bones than we do when we think of someone's bones. The word translated "bone" is *etsem*. Far more than "bone," *etsem* means "essence" or "substance." That means "Substance!" with a capital "S" and the "!". While we might consider it a bit disrespectful to kick a few bones around, the

Hebrews saw it about as bad as kicking the person around and cursing him into oblivion, as well!

Let me give you a few examples. In Genesis 29:14, Laban says almost the same thing as Adam said, to his nephew Jacob; *"Surely thou art my bone and my flesh"*(KJV). He meant, "You're Jewish. You're family. You're the same spiritual ancestry, human, and chosen of God."

When Joseph, in Egypt, was about to die, all he asked of the people he had saved from starvation was that when they finally left Egypt to go home, they would take his bones with them: *"And Joseph took an oath of the children of Israel, saying, God will surely visit you, and ye shall carry up my bones from hence"* (Genesis 50:25 KJV). Joseph wasn't simply concerned about his dry bones. There was much more involved than a mere sentimental desire that his remains stay with his people and rest in their own land. This concerned his spiritual essence, the "real him," still connected to those bones. He really wanted to go back home and stay in the Promised Land. If his bones went, he went.

This next example might tell it best.

> 1 Kings 13:21 *And it came to pass, as they were burying a man, that, behold, they spied a band of men; and they cast the man into the sepulcher of Elisha: and when the man was let down, and touched the bones of Elisha, he revived, and stood up on his feet.*

It wasn't the bare bones; it wasn't magic in the bones; it was that the real remains, the real essence of Elisha, a most powerful spirit and prophet of God, that was still resting there within the bones in his grave.

That's what I think Adam recognized in this woman and rejoiced in. He'd been through the "help-mate-preview-parade." He'd seen them all. None measured up like she did. She had the "right stuff," like his "stuff," and that's what God wanted him to recognize during the parade. I assume the "right stuff" was given to her by God, just as it had been given to Adam. He endowed the chosen female with the right stuff to make her right for the occasion and for His purposes.

Adam also says that she is flesh, like, or of, his flesh. In terms of the traditional rib story the picture is a little gruesome, but it would be accurate. I think it makes the most sense, however, with our new translation, and we might understand it as Adam rejoicing that she is thoroughly human! She is not chimpanzee or ape, nor some other non-fully-human creature. If we assume that the fossils scientists have recovered do come from other hominids and almost-human species, and even other humans, then our species appear to have a long history on earth.

There are numerous indications in the Scriptures, which we've been translating, that other men *(adam)* were at least contemporary with Adam, if not even preceding Adam. If there were other men ("mankind" could even include non-human hominids), it's highly possible they were living nearby, perhaps just outside the "enclosure" (the Garden). If so, then they, too, must have been represented in the parade. If we accept this set of possibilities, it is reasonable within our own interpretation, to understand that what Adam was saying was, "Aha, she is human *(adam)* like me, but even better, she is 'chosen' *(ha-adam)*. She is a child of God, too. She has Your Spirit, just like me!" It would confirm the obvious that when God selected *(laqach)* her, He breathed the same Spirit (or *demuwth?*) into her as well. She was then exactly like Adam in the qualities that mattered. That is why later, Genesis 3:20, Adam could say she was "the mother of all living." She was not the mother of all life, nor of all men, but of all Mankind—God's own special *bara* and *asah* Mankind.

When Adam named her "woman," he simply called her *ishshah*. *Ishshah* is another very indeterminate word as *adam* is. It can mean the minimum, "female;" or a step up from that, "female person;" or another step up, "woman" (a female of *Homo sapiens)*; or the greatest title, "wife." I think he meant to call her "wife," not just "woman." But that does create something of a problem if we don't go along with our own re-interpretation of verses 21 and 22 and the implications that there were other men on this earth, hominids or humans, but not *ha-adam* Men.

The problem is that Adam explains why he calls her the "woman" or the "wife" by saying it is "because she was taken out of Man." That surely points back to himself, doesn't it? It does, but only by ignoring another important bit of Hebrew linguistics. The King James Version cheats, I think, in capitalizing "man." So does the Revised Standard Version. The Living Bible stays truest to the original Hebrew wording when it uses "man." The "Man," you see, is not coming from *ha-adam,* or even from *adam.* As we've seen, *ha-adam* is the only word translating as Adam and is usually used when speaking of any of Adam's descendants! But here in verse 23, when Adam told us she "was taken out of man," he used *"iysh."* That's what is being erroneously translated as "Man," I believe.

It is true that *iysh* may translate "man." It often is used to refer to males of mankind. But it is also frequently used to express the mortal or non-spiritual, "non-*ha,*" aspect of man. It refers to the more biological (animal species) quality of mankind. It is also often used for wicked men (e.g., men of Sodom in Genesis 13:13; Cain in Genesis 4:1) and for those "mighty men and giants" being sired by "sons of God" who were illicitly taking daughters of *ha-adam* men in Genesis 6:4! So a careful translation of verse 23, "because she was taken out of man" also provides one more implication, at least, that Eve was "taken from mere men *(adam),*" not from Adam.

The underlying key to this interpretation, of course, is that there were other men *(adam)* living already when both Adam and Eve were chosen and transformed (about like being "born again") into *ha-adam.* That was the plan of Genesis 1:26 being completed.

That's quite a jump. If it is justified, do we land on any solid ground? Well, we can at least take another step forward and look at verse 24. It's consistent with that jump. Let's look at the same three versions again.

> Genesis 2:24 *Therefore shall a man leave his father and his mother, and shall cleave unto his wife: and they shall be one flesh.* (KJV)

> Genesis 2:24 *Therefore a man leaves his father and his mother and cleaves to his wife, and they become one flesh.* (RSV)

> Genesis 2:24 *This explains why a man leaves his father and mother and is joined to his wife in such a way that the two become one person.* (TLB)

No Bible scholars are absolutely certain whether Adam is still speaking here, or if Moses just editorialized, or what. Nonetheless, verse 24 announces a familiar dictum: *"Therefore shall a man leave his father and mother . . ."* (women leave, too, but remain more connected to their parents in the traditional Hebrew society). Isn't that a rather strange pronouncement either by, or to, a Man who has no father or mother? Or to a woman who has none, either? I have no doubt that God was the inspiration of the rule, but unless He gave Adam a great and vivid view of future generations and social institutions to come, it was still a meaningless point for Adam. Of course, it could have been instruction for the future when they had children of their own. But why should they be expected to "move out," at least for several generations? It seems verse 24 only makes good sense if Adam, or Eve, or both, did have biological ancestors they had left behind or outside (the Garden), when they were chosen, fashioned, or created, and given to each other in marriage (and not just a working partnership!).

Genesis 3:12 offers a measure of support to the thesis that Eve was brought from outside the Garden as a whole person. In Genesis 3:12, Adam and Eve have eaten the forbidden fruit. God asks of Adam, "Hast thou eaten . . .?" (KJV). Adam replies "The woman Thou gavest me . . ."(KJV). The New International Version says, "The woman you put here . . ." The Hebrew original is "the woman thou *nathan* me . . ." *Nathan* means "gave, ascribed, bestowed, delivered, gave over." The language never refers to "created" but agrees completely with the *laqach* (fetched for betrothal), which we saw was the Hebrew version of how she came into Adam's life. None of the language fits with the idea that Adam thought Eve was created, or removed, from himself

Genesis 2:25 offers a strong measure of support to the thesis that Adam and Eve were not alone but had friends and family nearby—or at least some human peers.

> Genesis 2:25 *And they were both naked, the man and his wife, and were not ashamed.*

It's beyond the reach of this study to be able to decide what it is that Adam and Eve got from God that transformed them to *ha-adam*. Verse 25 might, however, give us at least one more clue. It appears to have to do with this "naked" and "not ashamed." Alone, the verse seems rather trivial, an almost pointless piece of information. We need to connect it with Genesis 3:7

> Genesis 3:7 *And the eyes of them both were opened, and they knew that they were naked, and they sewed fig leaves together, and made themselves aprons.*

This verse indicates that something of what God originally gave them they had now lost. Once they sinned, once they broke trust with God and made a not-God choice, something that was intrinsic to their special place and gave them the benefits of verse 2:25 (no need, no shame), was lost. They were always naked, but suddenly in their own minds, in their own eyes, they became ashamed of that fact. What, exactly, that something is that made the difference is beyond the bounds of this study, but the events in these two verses do speak to the issues we are working on. They relate to the "shame."

The question is, what did it matter that Adam and Eve were unclothed if they were the only two humans on earth and there was no one else around to observe the fact? What would be the source of any other values or standards that would even suggest that there was shame associated with nudity? Shame, after all, is a relative sort of feeling and defined by societies. Look around the world, you'll see "proper covering" runs the gamut from a piece of jewelry, to only the eyes remaining uncovered. And God, as best I understand (for instance, King David danced naked unto the Lord), would not have been a source of shame to them over nudity. But, if they both came from a tribe where clothing was a fashion, and nudity was thought shameful, maybe even leading to problems like lust and social conflict, then we have a good answer. We'd have an even better explanation if hominid tribes, even tribes that they once knew, were near by and immediately able to see their undress.

Some folks (from a more conservative society) might still want to argue that being nude itself would have been shameful, and they just now could "see" it. But at least three answers come to my mind. One, few married adults are, or should be, ashamed of being nude around each other. Two, many peoples, even today, live half, or wholly, nude without any sense of shame. Three, Adam and Eve were living "before sin" and thus before shame. And the sin they committed (disobedience over the tree) was far from the sorts of things (fornication, adultery, lust) usually associated with nudity.

As always, a closer linguistic analysis also reveals interesting possibilities. In verse 25, Adam and Eve were "nude." The Hebrew word used is *arowm*. And they were not "ashamed," *buwsh*. More than "shame," *buwsh* means they were "not put to shame," "disappointed," or "disconcerted." Might that mean that, while in God's service and protection, even if they were without "proper" clothing or jewelry—by "outside" societal standards—they either did not hear or care about possible remarks or opinions of outside hominids? But once they chose not-God and put themselves outside their relationship with God, they now "heard" and heeded the "world"?

There's another clue in verse 3:7. The language there shifts just a little. What I called "nude" in 2:25 was from *arowm*. In 3:7, *arowm* is replaced by *erom*. *Erom*, too, is "nude," but there is a slight shadiness or color to it, which we might better catch in "naked." It's just a suggestive shade of meaning, but the fact is, *erom* is used throughout the Scriptures when there is immorality, or at least, "a lack of God's presence." One is "stripped," (*erom*) in acts of violence, or lust, or punishment. One is *erom* when depraved, fallen, or not even knowing better, i.e. knowing God. When God tells His servants to "clothe the *erom*," He means they are to bless them with more than just clothing that covers the body. So *arowm*, it seems, is at least a moral step above *erom*, which is itself a step above another word for definitely wicked nakedness, *ervah*. *Ervah* first appears when Noah is lewdly exposed before his disrespectful son's eyes. So you see, in those three Hebrew words, there is a scale of sorts, of something more than nudeness. It is almost a scale of distance from God, and it indicates some degree of moral slippage amongst God's own.

At first, Adam and Eve were simply naked. After their disobedience, they were more than simply naked. There was a moral element to it, almost as if others were judging them. And what happened when they "saw they were naked"? First there was shame. Then they covered themselves. Why would they cover themselves? Against whose eyes? And how?

The Scripture says they did it by immediately making a piece of clothing. That certainly suggests they had a pattern to copy and someone to copy it from. It's a type of clothing that we can see in many tropical forest tribes even today—aprons of sewn leaves. I suppose I might think of the leaf, but not of sewing it. Sewing itself is a social skill and involves a technology, which would be new to the Garden, by all reports. And what did God do? He replaced the leaves with furs, a real (hitherto immoral) step up. Did this "gift" of skin clothing serve to maintain some level of difference between his chosen and some other hominids? Could it even be a sign of superiority or sign of continuing favor and protection from God? Was it a sort of "Leave my chosen alone!" message for predators and other men? Is that what Cain feared he would lose when he was exiled? Questions like these seem to never end. But they are, at least, worth thinking about.

This is as far as we go in this book. You can take these new translations and ideas we've come up with and see how they fit with your understanding of this ever-living, ever-growing book called the Holy Bible. The last issue we've explored, whether there were other humans or other hominid species, co-existing with Adam and Eve, can, I think, answer a lot of other questions people wonder about. For instance, whom did the children of Adam and Eve marry? Who was Cain afraid of when he was sent into exile? Whom did God protect him against with the "mark," and who needed to hear the words of His proclamation of protection? With whom did Cain build a city? Who were the ones who so angered God by breaking some sort of rules in "taking" the daughters of Men?

However you choose to use this study, and whatever you choose to believe or not believe, I think you now at least have a lot more knowledge and understanding about the Creation. You don't have to duck or pretend to be out when the Evolutionists knock at your door, handing out tracts. Invite them in for a good debate. You're pretty well equipped now to win that debate.

Chart A

The Scientific Outline | The Genesis Outline

Years Ago (millions)	ERA	Period	ORIGINS by FOSSIL RECORD	MATCHING GENESIS VERSES
0	CENOZOIC	PRESENT TIME	First Hominids	Verses 1:26, 27
20				
40			First Monkeys, Apes	Verses 1:24, 25
60		65	Last Dinosaurs	
80			First Primates	
100	MESOZOIC	CRETACEOUS		
120			First Flowering Plants	Verses 1:11c, 12c
140		138		
160		JURASSIC	First Birds	Verse 1:21c
180				
200		193		
220		TRIASSIC		
		225	First Mammals	Verse 1:21b
240			First Dinosaurs	Verse 1:21a
260	PALAEOZOIC ERA	PERMIAN		
280		280		
300				
320		CARBONIFEROUS	Great Coal Forests	
340			Great Dragonflies	Verses 1:11b, 12b
		345	First Reptiles	Verse 1:20b
360				
380		DEVONIAN		
400		395	Lobe-fin Fishes	
			First Insects on Land	
420		SILURIAN	First Amphibians	
440		430	Fishes with Jaws	
460				
480		ORDOVICIAN	Plants on Land	
500		500		
520				
540		CAMBRIAN		
560				
580		570		
600	PRECAMBRIAN		Plants in Water	
			Invertebrate Animals	
			Algae, Seaweeds	Verse 1:20a
			First Living Things	Verses 1:11a, 12a

Chart B
Hypothesized Evolutionary Linkages": Where's the Proof?

This illustration is adapted from, *The Way Nature Works* (p. 137, Macmillan Publishing Company, NY, 1992, Robin Rees, Sr., Executive Editor). Its caption explained: "Tracing the origins of mammals depends on the availability of a good fossil record . . . possible lines of descent have been suggested." In other words, it supposedly shows the evolutionary history of mammals.

In the legend, the lines which "spiral out" from some purported common ancestor of about 200 million years age, were originally color-coded. Known fossil "sequences" (which are themselves imagined/theorized ancestral lineages; i.e., "evolutionary origins") were indicated in red-orange. "Proposed linkages" (they mean "evolving" lineages/linkages for which there are no fossil finds; i.e., "hopeful guesses," pure speculation) were indicated in orange. Let me tell you, only a very careful reader could detect the two colors separately, and almost everyone would look at the original and interpret it as showing the "evolutionary history" was pretty well documented and proven. Well, we have first cut the two lines apart, separating the red-orange "fossil record" from the orange "proposed linkages." We then "stippled" the orange (poked it full of holes). Now you can see that the evolutionary theory—the belief that all known mammals are evolved from one single ancestral species, starting some 200 million years ago—is not just still only a theory, but almost all the ancient fossil "shapes" which could at least be used to argue for it by filling in the missing "shapes gaps" haven't even been found. They are just assumed to have once existed. I think that those assumptions, artfully concealed in the original diagram, are well within the bounds of "reasonable doubt." The case for Evolution is far from proven!

To order additional copies of

Hey Mom, What About Dinosaurs?

send $12.95 plus shipping and handling to

Books Etc.
PO Box 4888
Seattle, WA 98104

or have your credit card ready and call

(800) 917-BOOK